# Blackinese

# Blackinese

*Reflections on Race and Ethnicity from a
Biracial Millennial*

**By Patricia Bradby Moore**

**Disclaimer:**
The viewpoints, events, and opinions expressed in this book are my own and are
based on my personal experiences, memories, and recollections. They reflect my
recollections and personal perspectives and may not represent universal truths or the
experiences of others. While every effort has been made to ensure accuracy, some
events, dialogue, and details may have been altered, condensed, or reconstructed
for narrative purposes. The content provided is intended solely for informational
and entertainment purposes. In some instances, names and identifying details have
been changed to protect the privacy of individuals, and any resemblance to actual
persons, living or dead, in those instances is purely coincidental. The institutions and
organizations mentioned in this book are referenced solely as part of the author's
personal experience. The views and opinions expressed are those of the author and do
not reflect the official policy or position of any institution or organization.

**Limitation of Liability:**
By reading this book, you agree that the author and publisher are not responsible for
any loss, injury, or damages that may occur as a result of following the advice or ideas
presented. The author and publisher disclaim any liability for any consequences that
arise from the use or misuse of the information contained in this book.

**Library of Congress Control Number:** 2025906607

**ISBN:**
Paperback: 979-8-9929998-0-8
Ebook: 979-8-9929998-1-5
Audiobook: 979-8-9929998-2-2
Published by: 804 Press

For more information, visit www.patriciabmoore.com

Cover design by: Megan Price
Editing by: Erika's Editing
Typesetting: Jana Burtner
Illustrations: Patricia B. Moore

*For anyone who has ever questioned where they fit in,
felt the pull of multiple worlds, or sought to make sense
of their own identity. May you find peace in knowing
that your story is a beautiful and essential part of
the larger narrative.*

# Contents

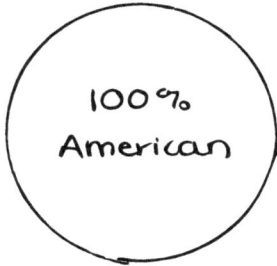

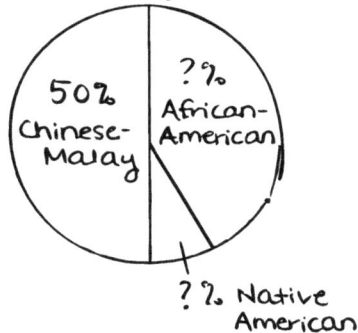

# Introduction

LIVING IN NEW YORK CITY during the early years of my adulthood was both beautifully inspiring and a true test of my survival instincts. When walking the city streets, it was typical for me to hear whistles and catcalls from male construction workers on the job. (I swear, that city will forever be under construction.) As I stepped out of my apartment, I would often slip my earbuds in beneath my bouncing black curls, slide oversized sunglasses over my almond-shaped eyes, and pretend to disappear—avoiding the need to respond to these men. It was quite fabulous. I never kept my music too loud because I felt a high volume was unsafe, especially when walking on sidewalks that run alongside speeding cars, crazy cab drivers, and cyclists with no regard for even the most standard and simple traffic laws. So, I kept my music at a level where I could still hear the city around me, but that didn't mean every person with the audacity to yell pickup lines at me needed to know it.

One day, I was in a hurry to meet some friends for brunch, and a guy passing by me on the sidewalk decided he wanted my attention. He said something to me as I briskly walked past, but I didn't bother to decipher the words coming out of his mouth—nor did I care enough to even slow down and try. It was obvious he didn't want anything but a boost to his own confidence, so I ignored him and continued on my way.

A few blocks later, I heard the same voice in the background of my music. As I turned around and tilted my sunglasses down to see exactly where this voice was coming from, I was not surprised to find the same young man following me down the street. When our eyes met, I instantly regretted tilting my sunglasses; now he knew I could hear him. Out of obligation to my guilt, I removed my earbuds. "Are you talking to me?" I asked, as if I didn't know. He then attempted to make small talk, but I quickly let him know I was in a hurry—if there wasn't anything I could help him with, I needed to be on my way. He then asked the question that almost every guy would ask after sixty seconds (or fewer) of conversation with me. "If you don't mind my asking, what are you?" My caramel complexion often conjures curiosity in people, so I gave him the same response I always gave: "I'm American." With that, I turned forward toward my destination and walked away.

The young man was persistent and kept following me. "Yes, I know that," he said. "But what *are* you?" My answer stayed the same. He obviously thought I didn't understand the question, because then he said, "Okay, I'm African American, and you are...?" No thanks to a red traffic light and a long string of cars, I was forced to stop in my path and finish this inane conversation. So I asked him, "Have you ever lived in Africa?" "No," he replied. "Then you're just American, too," I said as I put my earbuds back in and walked away.

It's not that I'm ashamed of my heritage or that I don't want people to know my ethnicity. I'm just annoyed at the amount of emphasis that's put on my racial and ethnic makeup. Genetically, I'm Asian, Black, and Native American, but I was born and raised in mainstream America. I'm American. At the time of my encounter with the young man, I had never been to any country in Asia, and I'd only spent a total of eight days in Africa on an educational trip—and at no point had I ever felt "at home." I wanted to identify as American and leave it at that.

As an American, when someone asks, "What is your ethnicity?" most likely your first instinct is not to respond with the country in which you were born and raised. Rather, you're likely to cite the countries or continent your ancestors came from before arriving in—or being brought to—the US. Because those in America often yearn to associate themselves with "their roots," they align themselves with countries they have probably never been to and/or cultures that they may have never truly experienced firsthand. Part of me doesn't understand this. Why not instead associate yourself with the culture you grew up in and are most familiar with, the culture that has genuinely made you who you are today?

The Oxford English Dictionary defines the word *ethnicity* as "the quality or fact of belonging to a population group or subgroup made up of people who share a common cultural background or descent." Those in America, with a few exceptions, all share a common culture, even if there are many subcultures within that culture, and it's *incredibly* common to take pride in being American. So, if almost everyone in the US is so "proud to be an American," why is American not considered an ethnicity in its own right?

These are questions I have spent decades of my life contemplating. *Who am I, really?* Although my father was born here, my mother was born and raised on the island of Penang off the coast of Malaysia. For this reason, I believed in my childhood that I was half Malay. In my late teenage years, I had a conversation with my older sister, who reminded me that my mother's mother is actually Chinese. My mother grew up in Malaysia, but her ethnic association was Chinese Malay, in the same way a Black person in America might be referred to as African American: Her cultural heritage was named first, and her country of birth followed thereafter. I felt then that if my mom was born and raised in Malaysia, it made her ethnicity Malay. In my view, it didn't matter where my grandma was from, and my mother has never even been to China.

As I've gotten older, I've come to realize that recognizing geographic origins does, in fact, matter to many people. It's a part of how they define themselves. Yet visiting or spending time in a specific geographic location does not necessarily make you more or less connected to the culture. If your heritage is Swedish, you can travel to Sweden, but that doesn't make you any "more Swedish." Culture is about customs, and those can be experienced anywhere.

My father is of African American and Native American descent. I couldn't even begin to try to tell you what percentage he is of which—and neither could he—but I know from the mouth of my own grandfather that those are the ethnicities that make up his ancestry. However, I'm not sure my dad associates with Native American culture at all, so why do the percentages matter? To my knowledge, no one in my family has been a member of a tribe for many generations. Despite growing up in southeastern Virginia, an area with active Native American tribes, I have never once heard my dad or his siblings speak of attending any Native American meetings or events, not even the annual Chickahominy Indian Tribe Fall Festival & Pow-Wow, which brings together many tribes from the area.

On the other hand, I have many memories of attending Union Baptist Church. Founded in 1862, Union Baptist Church was the third Black church established in my dad's home county. My dad's mother attended that church, starting at age eleven, and she was a faithful, active member until her passing at the age of ninety-one. I was always happy to accompany her to services because church was the place where she felt most at home, and I cherish the memories of us in worship together.

My dad's family extends far outside of the home he grew up in. As is typical in Black Southern culture, I had many aunts and uncles growing up that I'm sure are not related to me in any way, but who helped raise me as a family member would. Black culture is something I felt fully immersed in as a child, due in large part to the close-knit community my dad is a part of. It's his lived experience that would lead my dad to tell you he's decisively Black. I'm doubtful he would use the term *African American* unprompted, but we will get to my observations of this delineation later in the book.

Modern US culture is so obsessed with recording ethnic roots that this question of ethnic association is one I've always been constantly confronted with. When I was a kid, I must have greatly confused the Virginia Department of Education during their standardized testing. Back then, those silly Scantrons (or "bubble sheets," as I would call them) only let you mark one circle for race. I fell into three different categories, so out of fairness, I marked a different one each year. It wasn't until I reached high school that biracial and multiracial became options. This made me happy, and I still thought it was ridiculous we had to mark anything at all.

Due to my racially ambiguous features, my ethnic association is an external conversation and debate that's recurring in my life. It has also been a long-fought internal struggle: Only recently, in my adult years, have I come to peace with *all* the parts of my heritage. This was no small feat, but today I'm confident in who I am.

This book is an exploration of who I am and some of the events that have shaped me. It's a more-informed reflection on various moments in my life—moments that I may not have recognized as pivotal at the time, but that I now understand impacted the way I see myself and the world. I started writing this book at the age of twenty-three, and I'm glad it has taken me fifteen years to pick up the pieces and finish what I started. I've lived many exciting, meaningful experiences between then and now, and I've learned a lot.

At twenty-five, I moved to Malaysia, and that experience had a tremendous effect on the way I now navigate through the world. My time in graduate school and the many professional and personal experiences that followed have taught me so much, and I hope others might learn from and/or be comforted by my stories. I hope at least a few people out there see themselves reflected in the pages that follow.

I decided to finish this book after observing the increasing number of young people in the US who are multiracial. According to the 2020 census, among those who reported identifying as "Two or More Races," 32.5% were under the age of eighteen.

Between the 2010 and 2020 censuses, the multiracial population in the 18–44 age category increased by 300%.[1] The world is changing!

As the percentage of the US population that identifies as more than one race is growing rapidly, the amount of literature that covers the lived experience of multiracial people is still minimal. Growing up, I often felt isolated in my mental and emotional struggles as a multiracial and multiethnic kid. I only had my older sister—who was fielding the same uncertainties—for support.

Writing this memoir brings me joy, as it will offer today's multiracial youth a resource to help them feel less alone in their journeys of self-discovery. For those who have long faced challenges with being multiracial—or are still navigating them—this book is for you, too.

---

1    Rico, Brittany et al "2020 Census Shows Increase in Multiracial Population in All Age Categories," June 1, 2023, https://www.census.gov/library/stories/2023/06/nearly-a-third-reporting-two-or-more-races-under-18-in-2020.html

# PART I:

# CHILDHOOD

How far back is history?

Desegregation of schools
1960: Ruby Bridges (Age 6)
New Orleans, LA

1971: My Dad (Age 16)
Charles City County, VA

Oreo: A type of cookie
OR
Oreo: A derogatory term
for an African-American
who is presumed to have rejected
the values and traditions of their
race and ethnicity, and has instead
adopted the norms of dominant
European-American culture.
(Source: Urban Dictionary)

"You speak like a white person."
└ TRANSLATION ┐
"You speak using proper English."

why don't you have any Black friends?

Signs I am Asian:
☒ Speaks a dialect of Chinese
☒ Celebrates Chinese New Year
☒ Plays piano well
☑ Eats with chopsticks

You have that GOOD hair.

Durian: A fruit that taught me
smelly ≠ bad.
Thus increasing my willingness
to try different foods.

Which is correct?
• Eastern or western medicine
• Christianity or Buddhism

>>> Diverse friend groups ➔ Trying new things <<<

Steps to embracing my identity:
① Acknowledge my feelings toward myself (good or bad)
② For each negative thought, ask "Does this serve me?"
③ Express gratitude for my unique attributes.

# CHAPTER 1

# The Foundations of My Cultural Identity

## *Black*

COLORS ARE USED to describe things as they are observed. A banana is yellow; a pear is green; a strawberry is red. Based on the previous statements, I would describe the color of my skin as tan or maybe caramel. I know people who are beige and brown. We call people of African descent Black, but I've never known anyone who is black, like truly black. A deep, dark shade of brown, yes. But black, no.

Growing up, I recall associating people with colors far more than with ethnicities. White or black were really the only options. I had heard people refer to Native Americans as red and Asians as yellow, but neither of those made much sense to me. Granted, I didn't know many Asians outside of my own family, but I would never refer to my mother as being yellow. Her skin is beige with brown freckles; there is nothing yellow about her.

When I was young, a family friend shared with me a story about her trip to Thailand. All the locals there referred to each other as white. Our family friend, who is Caucasian and never kept much of a tan, was referred to as pink. I thought that was kind of clever. Pink is descriptive of what someone who is sunburned might look like, and since the likelihood of becoming sunburned in Thailand if you have fair skin is pretty high, pink seemed to me quite fitting as a term for Caucasian tourists.

I understand we need to use adjectives to describe one another. Color is an obvious feature that helps to describe the way one looks. What I could never understand is why we can't accurately assign them. If you were told to go pick out a black shirt at a store, most people would be confused if you brought back a brown one. However, if I asked you to point out a Black person in a room, no one would be confused when you pointed out a person with brown skin. Colors are the same regardless of the canvas, are they not?

This was my introduction to race in my formative years. It was less about shared ancestry and more about physical appearance—color, to be exact. Race was used to describe but also to separate, and it was a way to indicate otherness. Particularly as a kid, you don't want to be othered. You want to be included. So, race became a thing of negative association in my mind. While color may have been intended as a way of grouping people together, from my view as a person of color in a predominantly white town, it was instead used as a way to delineate and separate. So naturally, I wanted to avoid the topic whenever possible, to pretend race didn't exist. However, if you are a person of color in America, you know just as well as I do that this is an impossible task, because conversations about race are embedded in every facet of life as we know it. This country was built upon a socioeconomic hierarchy of race, and the ripple effects of that system are still evident—and, at times, inhibiting. But this is not a book about struggle, this is a book about perspective. In fact, this book is a collective of perspectives from inside the mind of a single individual who is black and yellow, yet who is still somehow expected to see the world through rose-colored glasses.

## History Is Not as Long Ago as You Think

I was well aware my paternal grandma worked for the Bennett family from the time I was a little girl. The Bennetts owned a small store down the road from my grandma's house, and my sister and I would visit the store to get chips and candy. Mr. and Mrs. Bennett were almost always there—the wife at the register, and the husband at the butcher counter in the back. They would greet us with warm smiles and sometimes sneak us samples of sliced country ham.

It wasn't until I was much older that I realized what working for the Bennetts truly meant for my grandma—and for me. When Mr. Bennett passed away, I attended the memorial service with my dad, and we waited in line to give our condolences to the family. As we shook hands and exchanged hugs with Mrs. Bennett and her children, they reminisced about the happy times with my grandma to make conversation. By this time, my grandma had passed, and while I had always felt protective of her, I felt—and still feel—that emotion even more strongly now that she lives on only through her legacy. One of the Bennett children—who are from my parents' generation—fondly remembered my grandma's cooking, especially her potato salad. That recipe was passed down to my mom and then to me, so when this woman asked if I would share the recipe with her, my mouth responded, "Of course," but my mind responded, "Who do you think you are?!"

It hadn't occurred to me before that moment that my grandma had helped raise the Bennett children in the same way she'd raised her own family. They knew her as I knew her, and something about that upset me. In an almost childlike way, I didn't want to share my grandma. Her love and care (along with her home cooking and recipes) should have been reserved for our family, or at least for people who were associated more closely with the rest of us. The Bennett children were not blood relatives or even play-cousins who showed up for family functions and holidays. They were people I only knew from afar.

A few months later, I was watching the film *The Help*, which is adapted from a book of the same name. I had read the book, and I'd even seen the movie before, so I knew the story is largely focused around two Black maids in the Deep South in the 1960s. But this time, when I watched, I began to cry uncontrollable tears. While the Bennetts were a wonderful family who treated my grandma as one of their own, until that moment I had not seen my grandma as a Black woman working for a white family in a county full of historic plantations. My grandma's house in Virginia was indeed surrounded by those plantations—in fact, there was even one across the road from the Bennett's store. She had grown up in that county, and she must have seen it as it was during those years, years that looked *very* different from modern times. Since my grandma didn't tell me much at all (or anything, really) about her formative years, I can only speculate about what she saw and her perspective from what I know of history.

My grandma worked for the Bennett family until I was in high school—to put that into perspective, I graduated in 2004. We saw her most Sundays when I was growing up, and when I left for college, I would call her every weekend. Until she passed, I talked to my grandma every Sunday of my adult life. When I moved overseas to Malaysia, I would still call her via Skype. No matter where I was in the world, I would call her on Sunday and listen to her tell me about church, her regular trips to the grocery store, and her hairdresser. She was without a doubt one of my best friends, and I wish I'd gotten her to open up more about her job and her childhood. I did ask, but she usually changed the subject.

In grade school, when we were reading about history, we would think about the events we studied as happening a long time ago, but some of our history isn't as old as we often expect. For instance, we might think segregation and Jim Crow are in the distant past, but my own father lived through America's Civil Rights Era. In fact, he was a sophomore in high school when his school district in Virginia was finally integrated. Looking back on the history lessons of my youth, I wish our teachers had assigned us to go to our parents and grandparents and ask them about events they'd lived through; we would have been given a more personal perspective on history, and our sense of time would have been reframed.

Part of what's interesting about being a child of more than one race is that when you talk to your family, you get a variety of perspectives. My mom didn't grow up in the US, so she can't tell me about integration, but she can still tell me about how she has seen race play a role in her life and in her society in Malaysia.

She can also share how the American Civil Rights era was perceived from an outsider's perspective. It's enlightening to ask questions of our loved ones because, by adding in the nuances of our heritages, we enrich our knowledge of historical events. Even though you might not see your family in the history books, you can sometimes bring history to life through conversations with your family.

## You Look Black

When I was in middle school, my mom enrolled me in a marine biology summer camp. This camp sent me down to the Outer Banks in North Carolina. To me, being at the beach was the greatest way to spend the summer! We spent a lot of time in the sun, and like most kids, sunscreen was not a priority for me when getting ready each day. I'm sure the counselors were aware sunscreen was necessary, but I'm not sure if they thought it was necessary for *me*. To set the record straight, just because there is a higher level of melanin in my skin does not mean I don't need sunscreen, and it certainly doesn't mean I won't get sunburned. It excites me today to see products like Black Girl Sunscreen, which helps drive home the point that we *all* need to protect our skin. However, that was not the norm in the years of my youth, and so I would always get a few shades darker in the summer.

That particular summer was the most time I had spent in the sun, cumulatively speaking, in my life, and I will never forget arriving back home on the bus to parent pickup. My sister walked toward me and said, "You look black! I told Mom that was you, but we almost didn't recognize you."

I tan pretty easily, but I lose that color almost as quickly as I gain it. (I'm not sure what that says about the melanin in my skin.) Growing up, because I performed a lot with a song and dance group, I had a kit full of stage makeup. I always had two sets of foundation—one for summer and one for winter—because my skin tone would change so drastically from the summer sun. In retrospect, I'm sure my makeup, including that extra foundation, was expensive for my parents because I couldn't use premixed foundation shades. I had to get custom-blended makeup, so we would visit the Prescriptives counter in the department store at the mall. We would have the people at the counter mix different shades of foundation and test them on my skin until they got something close enough to look natural. Then they would mix a full bottle of it for my mom to buy. Prescriptives built their brand on custom-blended foundation in the late 1980s and early 1990s, but by 2009, their parent company, Estée Lauder, shut them down due to lack of long-term viability, since a great number of new, pre-mixed shades were entering the market. Today, there is so much variety in makeup that it sounds ridiculous to have to pay to have your foundation custom blended, and I can now find a shade close enough to my skin tone in almost any brand without much effort. For me, the irony is now that such products are readily available, I barely ever wear them at all. I've learned that letting my skin breathe and drinking lots of water keeps my skin happy and reduces the need for makeup in the first place.

Even without having to switch between shades of foundation throughout the year now, I still notice when my skin is lighter in the winter and darker in the summer, but it's simply an observation with no emotion attached to it. When I was younger, though, it always felt like the grass was greener on whichever side of the spectrum I *wasn't* on at the time: In the winter, I wished I had more of a tan, while in the summer, I would worry I was getting too dark. Conflicting cultural messages were telling me that being too dark wasn't good, but then the booming business of tanning salons was telling me that being too light-skinned was also not ideal. So, the lesson there should have been: Culture doesn't know anything, and we should just be happy being who we are in any given moment. That's not the message I took away in my teens and early twenties, but it is how I live my life today. I just take comfort in being me.

Reaching this place of peace was a journey that required both conscious choice and gradual practice. Although I eventually learned to view my skin-tone fluctuations as mere observations rather than sources of anxiety or self-doubt, this shift didn't happen overnight; it involved a deliberate effort to detach emotions from my thoughts about my appearance. I had to keep reminding myself that my worth was not tied to how light or dark my skin was at any given moment. For anyone struggling with this kind of self-acceptance, I recommend starting with small steps. Acknowledge your feelings without judgment. Challenge negative thoughts by asking if they serve you. Focus on gratitude for your unique attributes. Over time, these practices can help cultivate a more accepting and peaceful mindset, allowing you to embrace who you are in every moment.

## Seemingly White

Personally, I don't actually remember facing many incidents of overt racism as a kid. I realized the number of minority children in my school was small, and I made a conscious effort to avoid discussing race. As a result, I never allowed myself to feel isolated because of my appearance or racial identity. As I grew older and traveled more, I realized that maybe I had experienced more incidents of racism than I'd originally thought—I had either chosen not to recognize them as such, or I'd simply lived in a state of ignorant bliss. In fact, it started to seem as if racism was sprinkled all throughout my childhood; it came in the form of Confederate flags flown, "Dixie" branded apparel, and language so colloquial—such as comments from the "peanut gallery" and sitting "Indian style" in grade school—that I never questioned it. (The reclaiming of the N-word in popular music during my coming of age certainly did *not* help). It seems crazy to say now, but at a young age, these flags, T-shirts, and colloquialisms meant nothing to me. They just were. So, until I was older, it didn't occur to me that these things could be (and, to many people, are) extremely offensive.

There are only two incidents from my childhood when I recall recognizing explicit racism in the moment. The first was the only time that I, as a child, was blatantly separated by my peers based on the color of my skin. I was in elementary school, and I was sitting outside with a group of my friends at recess. One boy, who I considered a friend (although we weren't close), decided to start the "White People Club." I wasn't sure what had sparked his idea, but I do remember feeling confused. The only "white people club" I had ever heard of was the Ku Klux Klan, and at such a young age, I only knew three things about them: They wore ghost costumes with cone-shaped hats that doubled as face masks; they would sometimes burn crosses; and most importantly, they hated Black people. In light of that limited yet striking knowledge, one would think my first instinct would have been fear—fear that my friends would start turning against me just because I was not of the same skin color. However, instead I felt confused as to why this boy couldn't just make up a club based on something we all liked and could enjoy together, like the game Heads Up, Seven Up.

The name of the club wasn't even what bothered me most. My *inclusion* in it was what bothered me, largely because it just furthered my confusion. The boy whose idea it was to start the club must have seen the puzzlement on my face, because he said to me, "Don't worry, you're in our club too. You're an Oreo, so you're practically one of us." I didn't know what that meant, but I felt a sense of relief in knowing I would be included. I later asked someone what it meant to be an "Oreo," because I wanted to know how I would fit into the White People Club. (I may be a combination of multiple races, but white is not one of them.) My friend explained that "Oreos are people who are Black on the outside but white on the inside." Still confused, I just said, "Cool."

Nothing ever became of the White People Club. In fact, I don't remember anything else being said about it after that day on the playground. I didn't ask about it, because that went against my instinct to avoid conversations about race. Maybe there were meetings I wasn't asked to be a part of, but I like to think the idea simply fizzled out, as most things do with young kids.

As an adult, I cannot believe I stayed quiet about my feelings towards the club. I'm not sure what actions would have been taken by the school in such a situation, but it's sad I didn't recognize in the moment that something was very wrong. I didn't mention to a single one of my friends that the whole situation was uncomfortable for me. Even now, I'm still confused by the term *Oreo* as a reference to a human being.

The second incident of blatant racism I remember encountering as a young person happened while I was out shopping at the mall in my teenage years. A middle-aged white woman walking with her preteen daughter stopped me and asked for directions. When I began speaking, the woman seemed taken aback. I asked her if something was wrong. She just stared at me and said, "Please don't take this the wrong way, but you speak like a white person." Contrary to her disclaimer, I took great offense, but I decided it wouldn't make me a better person to lecture this woman on how impolite and racist her comment was. After all, my parents taught me to respect my elders. So, I would never tell someone older than me that they didn't know right from wrong, and I especially wouldn't do it in front of a woman with a child who appeared to be at a very impressionable age. Instead, I ignored her comment, repeated the directions I had already given her, and then I continued on my way.

Looking back on that day, I again cannot believe I stayed silent. I don't know if that woman was referring to my accent, tone, word choice, or a combination of the three, but I have learned as I've gotten older that it's all too common in American culture for a well-spoken Black person to be described as "articulate." It's intended as a compliment to the individual, but use of the word *articulate* is rooted in the assumption that most Black people speak only African American English (also known as Ebonics), which is dialectical and considered by many as uneducated and unintelligent.

Referring to a Black person as articulate is an example of a microaggression. Microaggressions are the everyday, subtle—and oftentimes unintentional—interactions or behaviors that communicate some sort of bias toward historically marginalized groups. As rude as it would have been to correct an elder, I now feel it was more of an injustice to have not said anything to the woman in the mall, thus allowing her to perpetuate her behavior. By not speaking up, I may have had a part in inflicting that same scenario upon others who encountered the woman in the future. Not to mention, I was only doing a disservice to her daughter by allowing her to believe any Black person who speaks standard English is said to "speak like a white person."

Looking back, I can see how growing up in a predominantly white town and attending predominantly white institutions for both my undergraduate and graduate degrees served me well in certain ways, but coming up in largely white spaces was also a disservice to my growth in other ways. I was exposed to some amazing opportunities, both academic and extracurricular, as a result of the environments I grew up in. And while I am grateful for that, I also believe it prompted me to see the world through a lens of naivety. It also created subconscious biases in me that I was not aware of until later in life—biases I still have to actively work to recognize and combat. You can be a minority and still hold racial biases (even against your own race). We are likely all guilty of bias, but most are unaware of it. It's the awareness and active attempts to correct such biased mindsets and behaviors that truly matter.

## *Why Don't You Have Any Black Friends?*

I distinctly remember my dad asking me this question when I was in elementary school. I felt as if he were accusing me of deliberately choosing not to befriend any Black children. The reality was that most Black students at school weren't in my class. In our public school system, we were separated into honors and general classes at a very young age. I was sent down the honors path, and I had class with the same twenty or so students throughout most of my grade-school education. Unfortunately, most of the students in my class did not look like me.

In all fairness, most kids in the school didn't look like me. However, for the majority of minority students, their academic path looked different from mine. While I'm not positive race played a role in assigning students to one track or the other, the historical data tells us that student placement was likely colored by racial bias. There were only three other Black students I remember having class with; with all the other non-white students, I would only see them in the lunchroom or during extracurricular activities. It's hard to make friends with people you spend very little time with, but unfortunately, my dad's question stuck with me. As I've gotten older, I have been very intentional about keeping my friend-groups diverse.

As is the case for most people, not all of my friend-groups overlap or intersect. Sometimes I am the only Black person in one social circle or the only Asian person in another circle. In recent years, I have tried to be more intentional about bringing people out of their silos. A small way in which I do this is in my choice of children's books for friends who are becoming parents. As a kid, I always wanted more books with characters who looked like me, but all I remember getting was *Mufaro's Beautiful Daughters: An African Tale* by John Steptoe. There were so few books featuring girls of color back then. So now when I give children's books as gifts, I try to find ones that will diversify the bookshelves of my friends' children. Whether or not they are children of color doesn't matter, because it is important that *all* children see diversity in their books, their television shows, and their toys.

I wasn't one to play with Barbie dolls when I was young, but I remember the one time I asked for a Barbie for Christmas. That was the year I found out there was a Black Barbie, and that was the Barbie I wanted. Until recently, I really thought that was the year Mattel first came out with a Black Barbie, but apparently, she was launched in stores before I was even born—I just didn't come across her until I was about seven years old. (I guess, even at a young age, I wasn't buying into the idea of blonde hair and blue eyes being the only standard of female beauty.) So, since I never asked for Barbies or even wanted to play with them, it was an exciting moment when I suddenly took an interest. That year, I received three of the exact same Barbie—the Black Barbie— from three different family members for Christmas. They all understood representation matters. I might not have had many Black friends, but I did have Black dolls.

The irony is that the Black doll only partially represented who I was. I never had an Asian Barbie, and I don't know if there was one on the market at the time. Asian representation was scarce back then. I remember my sister reading *The Baby-Sitters Club* series, and there was an Asian character named Claudia. I immediately decided she was my favorite for no reason other than her appearance on the covers. I was not an avid reader and only read a few of the books in the series, but I still remember Claudia.

My dad never asked why I didn't have any Asian friends. My mom never asked, either. I guess they were both aware the Asian population in our county was almost non-existent, so it would seem like a silly question to ask. However, even when considering the distance between our immediate family and my mom's extended family on the West Coast, I'm sure I would have enjoyed having more Asian cultural influences in my life. It's not something I considered back then, but it's something I have thought about more as I've gotten older.

# CHAPTER 2

# Family Traditions, Food, and Religion

## *Importance of Community*

I OFTEN WONDER if I might feel differently about constantly having to explain my ethnic background if I felt more fully immersed in both of my family's cultures. My mom's family lives on the West Coast, while I was raised on the East Coast. We never celebrated holidays together, and I saw my mom's family only every few years. There also was no Chinese or Malay community in the town where I grew up, so there was no group in which I could immerse myself in Asian cultures and traditions.

My younger cousin, who grew up in California, was able to embrace our Asian heritage from an early age. Her parents—my aunt and her Caucasian husband—chose to connect her to her Asian roots, especially since my aunt had learned Mandarin in the army. My cousin was enrolled in a Chinese school at a young age, learning to read, speak, and write in Mandarin, and she also took part in the school's dance troupe. Her father (my uncle) took classes through the school for his own personal interest and to help encourage his daughter on her educational journey.

I watched the relationship between my cousin and her father strengthen through the years as they bonded over those immersive learning experiences and I felt a bit jealous—jealous because the opportunity to learn about Chinese culture was not presented to me, and jealous because my uncle took an interest in learning about his wife's culture, whereas my dad seemingly did not do the same with my mom. I had never heard my father ask my mother why she didn't cook more traditional Chinese meals, or why she never taught our family her native language. As I've gotten older, I have learned to let those jealous feelings go because my parents offered me so many other experiences, such as Girl Scouts, karate, cheerleading, pageantry, swim team, and the list goes on... My mother focused on giving me all the experiences she didn't have access to as a child, and that was special in its own way.

I now realize that my mother couldn't have shared any other languages with us because English became the only language she spoke fluently. I learned that she spoke Hokkien at home while growing up in Malaysia, not Mandarin or Cantonese. (I will revisit this later.) Since she moved to the US at the age of eighteen, her focus turned toward blending into American culture. The lack of practice speaking Hokkien—not even with family—made it more difficult to remember. I saw this in action when visiting her extended family in Malaysia while I was in my mid-twenties: My Mom could understand what her family members were saying, but she couldn't always remember the words needed to respond.

While my mom may not have signed me and my sister up for Chinese language lessons as kids, one of our extracurricular activities was somewhat stereotypical for Asian children: piano lessons. We didn't actually have a piano at home, but we did have a keyboard. I honestly don't remember where the idea of studying piano originated from, but what I do remember is not enjoying the lessons. I didn't make the time to practice like I should have, which made the lessons painful for both me and the instructor. My sister and I took piano weekly for a couple of years before we finally gave up the effort. Maybe it's a blessing we didn't live in an area with a heavier Asian population… it saved my mom from the embarrassment of my failure as a pianist.

Growing up, we didn't follow any Malaysian or Chinese holidays, so I wasn't connected to any Asian culture in that way. There is *one* time I remember celebrating Chinese New Year, which is the most important holiday in China and Chinese communities around the world. It celebrates the new year on the lunisolar calendar, which occurs on the new moon nearest the midpoint between the winter solstice and the spring equinox, falling sometime in late January or early-to-mid February. By "celebrate," I mean my grandma in California sent us the traditional little red envelopes with cash inside. I was excited to receive money at an unexpected time, but I was not very familiar with the traditions of the holiday. I knew the new year involved the rotation of the twelve Chinese zodiac signs, each of which is represented by a specific animal, because I'd learned this from placemats at Chinese restaurants. So for me, there was something important missing from the holiday even after receiving its most traditional gift (money). I was missing the holiday feeling you get inside when you celebrate with family and friends—that appreciation for the day itself and for the traditions that go along with it. I had no idea what Chinese New Year is all about, so instead of recognizing the holiday and all it stood for, my focus was on why we had never celebrated it before.

I later came to learn that the red envelopes are called *hóng-bāo* in Mandarin. In Chinese culture, the color red symbolizes good energy, happiness, and luck, so these envelopes are given as a goodwill gesture of prosperity at the new year. My favorite interpretation of this was expressed fairly recently by Malaysian comedian Ronny Chieng, who has a whole skit about how one of the traditional greetings on Chinese New Year—"*Gong xi fa cai*" (Mandarin) or "*Gong hay fat choy*" (Cantonese)—can be translated to mean, "I hope you get rich!"

Even today, I do not celebrate Chinese New Year, and I haven't learned to speak any Chinese languages. It has become apparent to me that actions such as these only hold value within the presence of a community. When you're exploring a new language, you need people to converse with to truly understand the practical application of words and phrases. When celebrating a certain holiday, you need people to celebrate with to breathe life into, and give heart to, the holiday. Fortunately, I now live in a city where these communities exist—it's just a matter of getting connected. Maybe in writing this book, I'll find the drive and inspiration to connect more closely with my Asian roots through my local community.

## Food Is a Universal Language

While I might not know all the cultural customs of my heritage, I do know food brings people together in any culture, and it unites people across cultures as well. One of the most fun parts of growing up in a multiracial family is the diversity, and contrast, of culinary dishes—each side of the family has its own traditional foods. Both Asian cuisine and Black Southern cuisine (commonly referred to as "soul food") graced our plates. Big family gatherings had both fried rice and fried chicken on the table, and we all felt more blessed for it.

My mom has never really felt drawn to the kitchen, but there are a few dishes she has perfected and makes on rotation. Then there are a few special-occasion dishes we all look forward to when a family gathering is added to the calendar. Her fried rice is one of those dishes. It's unlike any you will get in a restaurant, and while I know all the ingredients, I still can't seem to replicate it. It has eggs, shrimp, Chinese sausage, peas, carrots, and more. (I can't give away all her secrets.) I don't even like peas, but I will eat them in this dish. I remember Mom once made her fried rice for my whole class when I was in elementary school, maybe in first grade. She arranged it with my teacher in advance and brought in chopsticks, each pair held together on one end with a rubber band, to try to teach my classmates how to eat with them. Looking back, it was super ambitious to attempt to teach small children to eat with chopsticks, especially as we were eating rice, which can be hard for novice users to pick up and navigate into their mouths.

Another dish I always look forward to is one we refer to as "soy sauce chicken." I honestly think my mom just made up this recipe. It's a simple dish that only requires you to throw all the ingredients in a pot to boil for about forty-five minutes. I have never eaten anything like it elsewhere, and the flavor brings back happy memories every time. Just the scent wafting through the kitchen brings me joy. Due to the dish's simplicity, this is one meal I've been able to make many times on my own: It's cheap, easy, and delicious. I don't think my mom ever intended for it to be a recipe important enough to pass down to her children, but since the number of Asian-influenced dishes she makes is limited, each one has a special place in my memory.

A dish I'm *sure* my mom invented is what I refer to as "rice porridge." It's kind of like congee, but it's made with less traditional ingredients. My sister and I had braces growing up, and this is the dish Mom would make for us after we would get them tightened and couldn't comfortably chew. It was a one-pot meal made in the rice cooker: Mom would put ground turkey in for the protein and chopped celery for a vegetable. We would flavor it with soy sauce and eat it with a spoon. So satisfyingly delicious.

Both my grandmas loved to cook. I have fond memories in the kitchen with my father's mother, learning not to "shake 'n bake," but to shake and fry instead. We would put our chicken in a brown paper bag with flour, salt, and pepper before frying it in a heavy cast-iron skillet. We would also whip mashed potatoes with more butter than I'll ever admit, but if you had tasted them, you would understand the extra calories were well worth it. The smell of roast beef in the oven and collard greens in a pot atop the stove will forever live in my memory. It was the smell of Sunday dinners and grandma's love.

While I spent less time with my mother's mother due to the distance that separated us, I also have fond memories of her in the kitchen. She would soak dried shiitake mushrooms for hours before we were to start cooking. I remember sitting on the floor so we would have more space to wrap *nasi lemak* in banana leaves; *nasi lemak* is a traditional Malaysian dish made of coconut rice and served with chili paste, dried anchovies, cucumber, egg, and peanuts. She also taught me to make Japanese *maki* sushi rolls and spam *musubi* like her mother-in-law had taught her. My grandfather (my mother's stepdad) is Japanese American, and while I didn't get to experience this firsthand, I'm told his mother's cooking was some of the best this world had to offer.

Beyond the kitchen, my maternal grandma loved to garden. Not only did she grow beautiful flowers, but she also had multiple dragon fruit plants. She would pollinate these plants herself with a makeup brush since they aren't native to California's ecosystem, and it worked! It was so exciting when she would bring the fruits inside and cut them open—would they be purple or white inside? No matter what the outcome, both were delicious. She also had a persimmon tree from which she would take the fruits, slice them, and dehydrate them. She would send us home with gallon-sized Ziploc bags full of dried persimmons. At the time, dragon fruit and persimmon were exotic fruits that we would never see in the grocery stores at home. They were special to grandma's house.

The smells coming from grandma's kitchen on the West Coast were very different from the smells coming from my grandma's kitchen on the East Coast. Asian cooking uses ingredients that the average American nose may be a bit sensitive to. My maternal grandma used to make medicinal mushroom tea that she would heat on low in a large crock pot. The smell took some getting used to, but if you had a headache, this tea was magic. She also had plastic jars of tiny, dried shrimp that she would add to any vegetable dish without hesitation. I can't tell you the number of times I would see green beans or bok choy (two of my favorite vegetables) cooking in the pan, only to later feel a wave of disappointment as I scooped some onto my plate and found their flavor had been tainted by the dried shrimp. As you might imagine, cooking with dried seafood also added to the mix of scents wafting through the house from the kitchen. It was a smell I had to readjust to every time we would visit, but I wonder if I would internalize those particular scents differently if I had grown up in California with my mom's people. Those smells still conjure up fond memories for me, but since many of the dishes were not ones I ate regularly as a kid, that association is less one of intimate familiarity and more representative of specific cherished moments.

My comfort with strong food smells has served me well through the years. It has allowed me to try, without prejudgment, many different cuisines and unique dishes throughout my travels around the world. For instance, nothing has ever been more repulsive to me than the stink of durian, a notoriously smelly fruit, but I also enjoy the taste of durian fresh from the shell. It has a creamy, pillowy texture that you can't quite explain. You can only know it by trying it.

The first time I had durian fruit, we were actually at home in Virginia. Richmond only had one Asian grocery store at the time, and Mom took us there. When we saw they had fresh durian in stock, she decided it would be fun for us to try it. This was a fruit she had eaten and enjoyed as a kid, and she wanted to share that experience with us. I found the durian's spiky shell intriguing, but I had no idea what we were in for. The next day, after waiting for my dad to leave for work (He worked second shift, so he would leave the house around 2:00 p.m. and return somewhere between 11:00 p.m. and midnight.), my mom proceeded to prop the door open and throw open every window in the house as soon as his truck left the driveway. Then she used a large knife to tap the bottom of each durian right along the seam. This gave her the space to then stick the knife far down enough into that shell, with a quick twist of the blade, she could pull it apart. Despite doing this activity near an open door, the smell immediately took over the entire first floor of the house. We ate and enjoyed, then put what remained in the freezer (which helps to kill the smell). The windows and doors stayed open all day to air out the scent. My mom sealed the house back up just before my dad pulled into the yard late that evening, and I will never forget the moment he opened the door to walk into the house. The look on his face was priceless as he wrinkled up his nose and asked, "What's that smell?!" Thus, a warning to those who are interested in trying durian fruit: Pick a day when the weather is nice and open the durian outdoors.

To be fair, strange smells resulted from culinary delicacies on both sides of the family. When pig's feet or chitlins were on the stove at my paternal grandma's house, you knew it as soon as you stepped onto the porch. Usually, there was apple cider vinegar involved, which only added to the odor. The sulfurous smell of collard greens with ham hock simmering in a pot is another scent that might not appeal to everyone, but for me it's a signal to my nose that something delicious is in my future.

Now, we've been talking about foods that have strange smells, but there are also some foods that, additionally, are not so visually appealing. In my family, there was zero tolerance for picky eaters, so if you wanted to eat, you would eat whatever was put on the table. Neither pig's feet nor chitlins were my favorite, but being forced to eat diverse foods made me an adventurous eater from a young age. My paternal grandfather and uncles were avid hunters, so I also grew up eating venison as well as rabbit. I even had frog legs once or twice.

This openness to trying different things on my plate as a child may seem trivial, but it built a foundation of curiosity in me that has helped me be more inclusive in all that I do. I get excited to learn about and try new things. I am inquisitive instead of judgmental when it comes to things that are unfamiliar, and I have my diverse upbringing to thank for it. To me, no food is "weird," just different. And different isn't bad or scary; different is just an opportunity to potentially like something new.

## Medicinal Remedies

Western medicine is thought to be the most scientifically advanced system for treating illness, and thus the most effective. We are trained through American culture to visit the doctor annually, and to treat our ailments with pills, liquids, and creams, whether they are over the counter or by prescription. The cost of treatment using Western medicine can be very pricey, but we trust the cost will be worth the benefit. Now, I'm not saying we shouldn't trust Western medicine, but I wish to point out that there are alternatives.

The main alternative to Western medicine is Eastern medicine, which is thousands of years old and rooted in holistic principles that emphasize balance and harmony within the body. This approach often incorporates practices such as acupuncture, herbal remedies, and mindfulness techniques, all of which are aimed at treating the individual as a whole rather than merely addressing their symptoms. My mom's mother grew up in this tradition of more natural approaches to wellness, and moving to the US did not change that.

Trusting Eastern medicine is something I likely would not have thought to consider if it weren't for my maternal grandma. She didn't trust Western medicine, and she often had her own ideas about remedies to heal or cure ailments. The previously mentioned medicinal tea for headaches is one example of this. It had a strong, earthy, and pungent scent to it, which I took as a sign it must work—certainly, no one would voluntarily drink this tea if they didn't really believe it had healing properties. She also had a travel solution for curing headaches: She kept an ointment in a tube that was about the size of my ChapStick, and she would sniff it when her head was hurting. I believe the ointment was mentholated, but I never tried it myself.

Her approach to more natural remedies was in high contrast to my paternal grandma, who regularly visited her (Western) doctor and had all the pills to prove it. My paternal grandfather was the same way. Various health issues have claimed the lives of three of my grandparents, and I often wonder if they might still be here today, or if they would have suffered less in their last days, had we found some middle ground between Eastern and Western medicine.

# Religion

Faith has always been an important part of my life. I grew up in the church, the Southern Black Baptist Church, to be exact. My mom made sure our family attended church together on Sundays, and my sister and I participated in Sunday Bible school, vacation Bible school in the summer, and youth choir. (Our choir was called the Rainbow Brites.) My sister and I were baptized during our elementary school years by our own choice. I'm not sure if I really understood the full importance of baptism back then, but I loved church and I loved the Lord, so getting baptized seemed like the right decision. I still think it was, and I'm glad I did it, but I also acknowledge part of my decision at such a young age was likely just a sense of duty and/or a longing to be included.

My paternal grandma attended the same church for eighty years. She was a member of Union Baptist Church (UBC) in Charles City, VA, which was established in 1862 in the midst of the Civil War. It was founded as the third Black church in the county, and the roots of the congregation run deep, as does their passion for Christ. I remember UBC well. Their choir was small but mighty, and the music was *the best*. But the music was second in my mind to the outfits. Church fashion in Charles City County was *a must*, with a variety of beautiful hats always on display. The idea of wearing one's Sunday best seemed to have been invented there. Suits of all colors and shoes of all textures were shown off as members of the congregation strutted up and down the aisles before, after, and even—when the music so moved them—during services. It was and remains a church of community and tradition. They loved my grandma, and my grandma loved that church, and so I loved being there with her.

All through my life, as I've moved from city to city, I have made it a point to find a church home. My faith is important, and having a community to support me spiritually is a big part of fostering my faith. Since I've lived in so many places, I've now seen Christian worship approached in a variety of ways. I went from a very traditional church experience in my youth to a more modern, casual church experience in my early adulthood. When I was in New York City, a friend from college took me to her non-denominational Christian church, which was something I'd never heard of. It was *so* different from going to church with my grandma. You could even wear jeans!

I liked the style of the sermons in the non-denominational church, which tied Biblical teachings to modern-day experiences. The church bulletins were not for announcements but for note taking, with fill-in-the-blank-style notes. (Imagine a Mad Libs sheet, but instead of filling in random words in the indicated places, the pastor gave you the exact words to write on each line. This ensured everyone walked away with the same key takeaways and that the message was clear.) I became a member of that church shortly thereafter, and when my sister moved to New York City, she joined me and became a member. When I later moved to Austin for graduate school and to Los Angeles after that, I sought out similar church experiences, and luckily, I found church homes that suited me well.

Today, I attend a non-denominational church with a pastor who is a few years younger than I am. Now, this is church in a whole new way for me. The church has young, vibrant leadership and a tagline of "impacting culture through the innovative presentation of Christianity." The sermons are not only relatable, but there are props and theatrical illustrations that sometimes involve pulling churchgoers out of their seats and onto the stage. It's so engaging even my husband, a non-believer, will attend with me for the life lessons in the content and the theatrics.

I am a believer in Christ and always have been, but this doesn't mean I don't struggle with my faith. The Christian faith teaches the only way to heaven is through Jesus Christ, but I'm not sure I believe that, at least not totally. Both of my grandmas were women of faith—different faiths, that is—and both are no longer with us in this world. I have no doubt my paternal grandma is watching over me from heaven, and I also believe my maternal grandma is doing the same. My conundrum here is that my father's mother was baptized and believed in Jesus Christ, while my mother's mother was Buddhist. Buddhism is a faith that believes in a cycle of life, death, and rebirth. So, in that vein, I like to believe my Buddhist grandma's spirit lives on and that she watches over me in that way.

I do wonder if my faith would have been different had I grown up closer to my maternal grandparents. I know my dad's family, who are all strong believers in Christ, heavily shaped who I am and what I believe, and even my mom came to know Christ through my father and his family. Proximity is everything, and I sometimes wish I had asked to go to temple with my mom's mom while we were visiting with her. It was not until her passing that I had any temple experience, and even that experience was done virtually via Zoom.

This mismatch of beliefs from two people I hold dear to my heart makes me hope that, in the end, all religions are actually based around the same universal truths. I can't claim one grandmother knew better than the other; their faiths were based on how they were raised. Each of them was a remarkable woman who has left a legacy of love and kindness, and it's that similarity that makes them more alike than different. It's that similarity that leads me to believe they were both following faith in the right direction.

# CHAPTER 3

# Navigating Adolescence

## *Do You Shave Your Arms?*

THERE ARE CERTAIN traits I've inherited from each parent that I am thankful for. On my dad's side, one trait I value greatly is what Black girls growing up used to refer to as "that good hair." Black hair can be very kinky and tightly curled, which makes it particularly challenging to style and care for. As a result, hair-smoothing practices will often involve heat styling tools and chemical treatments that can cause discomfort or long-term damage if not used properly. But for me, I never had to use a relaxer or perm in my hair to tame the curls and frizz. The texture of my hair has always been fairly smooth, and it's easy enough to style, making it "that good hair."

From my mother's side, I inherited the trait of having very little body hair, which is common among people of Asian descent. My mother has never shaved her legs, and you would never know. Unfortunately, I wasn't lucky enough to be *that* hairless—I do have to shave my legs, but the hairs are extremely fine and grow slowly. My arms, on the other hand, have never grown any hair, so growing up other kids asked if I shaved my arms, which I've never done even once. As a child, I likely wouldn't have noticed my lack of arm hair if others hadn't pointed it out to me.

Having worked in concerts and music festivals early in my career, I found having no arm hair convenient for an odd reason. The number of events I worked at or attended that required one of those paper wristbands that affix with adhesive is more than I could ever count. The sticky part of the wristband is supposed to go over the inside of the wrist, where most people are hairless. However, I have heard from those with hairier arms that if you don't position your wrist correctly when asked by security to put your arm out for wristbanding, the adhesive can get caught in your arm hair, which can be both annoying and painful.

Hairless arms may seem insignificant, yet it's something multiple children brought to my attention on several occasions growing up. We are taught to see the differences in others, and I'm not implying that this attention to detail is good or bad. What I hope to communicate is that the traits that make us different also make us special. And different can be advantageous, depending on the circumstances.

Unfortunately, special can be hard to see sometimes, particularly at first glance. I once saw a meme which explained how an item's value is determined by a buyer. For example, if you have an old clock and try to sell it at a flea market, it might be worth ten dollars. However, if you were to take the clock to an antiques dealer, it could possibly be sold for hundreds or thousands of dollars, depending on where, when, and by whom it was made. The knowledge about and the appreciation for the item on the part of the buyer is what gives it value. In the same way, we as humans feel more valued in environments where others take the time to get to know us and appreciate us for who we truly are and not just who we appear to be.

The questions I received about my lack of arm hair as a child were not malicious, but they *were* othering. They made me feel different. It wasn't until later in life, when I found an environment where this trait worked to my advantage, that I came to appreciate being different. It's something so small, but even the little things matter.

## Shirley Temple Curls

In small-town Virginia, I was the only girl in school with hair like mine. "Shirley Temple curls," the school secretary would always say when I would swing by the main office for various reasons throughout the day. That always made me smile. When I moved to New York City to attend New York University (NYU), I was disappointed to find I was no longer the only curly girl in town. Long curls, short curls, black curls, brown curls, blonde curls, and just about any and every other kind of curl one could imagine were represented. Something that used to make me feel special suddenly felt very normal and lackluster.

Don't get me wrong, I do not now, nor have I ever, defined myself by my curls. In the words of India.Arie, "I am not my hair." However, my curls were one of my defining qualities growing up. When both girls my own age and older Black women would say to me, "You have that good hair," I took it as a compliment, although I didn't really know why. I never truly understood what that meant until one day during my freshman year of high school when I was at track practice, and it began to drizzle. One of the senior girls, an African American, was running around the track when I saw her run out of her lane and over to the sidelines, near to where I was stretching. She said matter-of-factly, "Now coach, you know Black people don't do rain!" The tone of the girl's voice and the look on her face made it seem as though she were joking, but it was obvious there was a hint of truth in the statement. (Rain can ruin a Black person's hairstyle, especially if they use relaxers or have a permanent.) At this point, I looked around the track and saw discontent on the face of every Black girl on the team, while all the white girls on the team continued to run through the drizzle as if nothing had changed. The remainder of practice was spent in the weight room.

I always liked it when it rained, personally. As a kid, I thought my hair looked better when wet, because when it was dry, it was always somewhat frizzy. I used to put gel in my hair after I got out of the shower to tame the "wispies," as my sister and I called them. The gel helped my hair look wet, and my goal was to always look as though I'd just stepped out of the shower.

The first time I ever straightened my hair, I felt like I was wearing a costume on Halloween. I looked so different it was almost like I wasn't myself. I liked the change. I didn't like how long it took to blow-dry my curls smooth, starting with the hair dryer and then having to go over small sections at a time with the flat iron. But the change was worth the effort, I felt, even if it took a lot of time to do at home.

It's worth noting here that, as a child and teen, getting my hair done at the salon was never an activity I enjoyed. Every hairstylist I went to had no regard for the pain she caused when her comb made its way through the tangle of my curls. My mother was the only person who was ever gentle on my curls, but unfortunately, she was not licensed to cut hair, nor was she well-versed in styling techniques to put my hair up for special occasions once I reached a certain age. In fact, there were a number of years when she regularly took me and my sister to get our hair professionally braided, with beads on the ends to hold things in place. Because braids can last up to six weeks, it simplified the process of getting us ready each morning, since she didn't have to deal with our hair on a day-to-day basis at all.

I may have had "Shirley Temple curls," but they, like my hairless arms, were yet another trait that separated me from my peers. When I attended sleepovers as a kid, I would watch the other girls play with each other's hair and teach one another how to do French braids. This was not an activity I could participate in, either because my hair was braided in cornrows or because it was simply too tangled and frizzy. With my mother being the only adult who was ever gentle with my hair, I certainly wasn't going to let a kid try their hand at getting a comb through my curls. To this day I still can't French braid my own hair, which I chalk up to the lack of practice as a young girl.

My hair set me apart when it came to cheerleading, too. I was a cheerleader from Pee Wee league through high school, and I always wanted to wear the same hair-bows the other girls wore. I did manage that, but my mother and I would have to find creative ways to incorporate the bows into my hairstyle. When it came to competition cheerleading in high school, we really had to get imaginative, because every girl on the mat was supposed to look the same—same uniform, same makeup, same hairstyle, same bows.

Sometimes crafting this uniform look required straightening my hair before styling it, and every time I did it, it required more hair products than any single person should use at one time. It also required twice the normal amount of heat on my hair, since I needed to blow out my natural curls before using a curling iron to replace them with uniform curls. And then came the copious amounts of hairspray. To be fair, all the girls on my team were using tons of hairspray to ensure their hairstyles would survive all the tumbling, stunts, and sweat that the day ahead would entail. All I know is that when we would watch, as a matter of tradition, the cheerleading film *Bring It On* the night before a competition, the other girls would be lined up and busy rolling one another's hair in curlers. I, on the other hand, would either sit out of the line or sit at the end of the line only to be helping someone else with their hair, while having no one putting rollers in mine. It was much like when I went to sleepovers as a child. This was a minor thing the other girls probably didn't think much of, but it mattered to me.

During my teen years, I would get my hair blown out at the salon for special occasions only (like cheerleading competitions). Meanwhile, my sister got a relaxer to put in her hair, and my mom bought her a Helen of Troy hair straightener so she could straighten her hair herself every day before school. I was quite jealous, because what little sister doesn't want everything her older sister has? My mom explained my sister's hair was thicker and harder to handle, which is why she was allowed to use a relaxer. I, on the contrary, have very fine, thin hair. My hair was not a hassle, and so my mom believed I shouldn't mess up my "Shirley Temple curls" for no reason.

## Curly vs. Straight

My mother encouraged me to keep my hair curly, except for special occasions, until I was in my late teens. Then, like any other rebellious youth, I went away to college and did exactly what my parents told me not to do: I bought a flat iron. After all, now there were tons of curly-haired girls all around, and my curls no longer made me stand out, so it was a good time for a change.

Now, I'm going to be completely honest with you: The CHI flat iron changed my life. It left my hair silky and smooth, and it shined *just* like in a Vidal Sassoon commercial. I wore my hair straight every day for months, as I felt it made me look older. The heat was hard on my hair, though, and eventually, using the flat iron dried out my scalp. It also killed the ends of my hair to the point where I had to cut off five inches of length to restore my tresses to a state of good health.

I had become so accustomed to my straight hair that I didn't want to go back to my curls. And, trust me, the curls didn't want to come back to me, either. My once-bouncy curls were now just messy waves. The shorter of my layers couldn't decide if they were curly or straight. My longer pieces wanted to curl, but about four inches out from my scalp, my locks seemed to get confused, and my curls began to lose their shape and just go any which way they pleased. Eventually, I dropped New York City salon money (read: more money than I *ever* thought I would) at a place that specialized in curly hair, and a couple hundred dollars later, I felt my curls were finally beginning to remember how to take shape.

The dilemma I then began to face was when to wear my hair curly and when to straighten it. It was obvious I couldn't let an appliance as amazing as the CHI just go to waste. So, I would go a few days straight, and then a few days curly, another few days straight, and another few days curly.

Over time, I have learned the versatility of my hair is a beautiful thing. I can do lots of things with it easily enough, unlike many girls of African descent. By my mid-to-late twenties, I had learned to wear my hair almost like an accessory—I had "curly hair outfits" and "straight hair outfits," outfits which complemented the hairstyle I chose on any given day. Plus, the ability to reproduce those teenage cheerleading hairstyles on my own had finally paid off. My determined mindset—yes, I *can* make my hair do anything I want—allowed me to learn to copy just about any up-do hairstyle, except for French braids, for special occasions. This was especially helpful in the years when all my girlfriends were getting married; doing my own hair, as opposed to using wedding hairstylists, saved me lots of money whenever I was a bridesmaid. This skill also proved helpful during my years working as a freelance event coordinator in New York City. The numerous fancy events I worked at or attended called for an array of sophisticated hairstyles, all of which I could create myself.

These days, I still keep a flat iron under my bathroom sink, but I rarely use it. Years of heat on my hair thinned it out even more, and in an effort to keep some hair on my head, I have learned to embrace my curls full time. The hunt for the perfect hair products still continues, but I imagine many people, regardless of race, struggle with finding products that work well for their hair. When I was a child, my mom used Luster's Pink Lotion on our hair, which I'm still not sure was intended for my hair's texture, but back then there weren't really any products being made for looser curls. Today, there are whole sections in the beauty aisles for curly hair of all kinds. Over the years, I have come to find my curls are somewhere between 3a and 3b on the Andre Walker Hair Typing System chart, meaning my curls are loose spirals. The fact that there are now charts to define curl types that can help curly haired people find the right products and styles for their hair reflects tremendous progress in the beauty world. It's now a wonderful time for curls!

## A Fish Out of Water

Something I never understood is the concept of tanning. In a world where it seems to work against you to have darker skin, there was a real obsession with tanning among my white peers when I was a teenager. (I even had one friend whose mom bought a tanning bed to put in their house.) Before going to the beach, girls would make an appointment at the tanning salon to create what they called their "base tan." I believe the purpose of this was to be able to spend more time in the sun at the beach without getting sunburned.

If I went with girlfriends to the beach, they would spend most of those hours lying on their towels in the sun. At the pool, they would also spend more time soaking up the sun in their lounge chairs rather than enjoying the cool water of the pool. I, on the other hand, love being in the water. I always have. Also, I had (and still have) no interest in lying in the sun for long periods of time: At a baseline, I am already tan, and skin cancer is a fate I don't want to tempt.

There seems to be a fine line between appearing tan and appearing Black or brown. On the one hand, I didn't want to spend too much time in the sun and get too dark, especially as a teenager. On the other hand, I didn't need the sun's help to create a more golden complexion, which is what the other girls seemed to be seeking. So, my multiracial background put me ahead of the curve when it came to keeping up appearances in the summer, a strange but welcome privilege if it meant one less thing to worry about as a young girl just trying to fit in.

Many of my school friends joined the local pool's swim team when I was in elementary school, and as a result, so did my sister and I. The pool was definitely a place where we were the only people of color. We always wore our swim team's caps to protect our hair. Our braids and beads would get swept up into our caps, and we would dive into the water like little fish being released back into the pond.

This year I learned Howard University is the only historically Black college or university (HBCU) with a swim team, thus making them America's only all-Black college swim team.[2] This matters because water sports are not usually seen as particularly inclusive. In fact, according to the Centers for Disease Control and Prevention, Black children ages 5–19 years old are 5.5 times more likely to drown than their white counterparts.[3] This is due, in part, to racial disparities of the past. During the Jim Crow era, public swimming pools were heavily segregated,

---

2    Fenno, N. (2023, February 1). Howard Swimming Is Making Waves in College Sports. Sports Illustrated. https://www.si.com/college/2023/02/01/howard-swimming-daily-cover

3    Centers for Disease Control and Prevention (CDC). (2014). Racial/Ethnic Disparities in Fatal Unintentional Drowning Among Persons Aged ≤29 Years — United States, 1999–2010. Morbidity and Mortality Weekly Report, 63(19), 421-426.

with many facilities designated as "whites only" spaces. This systematic denial of access to pools for Black Americans, coupled with violent resistance to integration efforts, contributed to the perpetuation of the false stereotype that "Black people don't swim." It's not necessarily a lack of interest or ability that has impeded them, but instead a lack of exposure and skill-building.

I live in a predominantly Black neighborhood today, and the public pool that's walking distance from my house can sometimes feel like my own private pool in the summer. There's not much activity there, and it's a wonder because the pool sits behind a community center where I see lots of children playing basketball and football. I'd love to see the pool bustling with activity in the same manner as the courts and fields.

I hadn't really thought about it until I started writing this book, but swimming is also not particularly popular among Asian Americans. According to a report by USA Swimming in 2017, 66% of Asian Americans don't know how to swim.[4] Cultural norms emphasizing modesty, particularly for women, along with a lack of emphasis on swimming as a recreational activity in many Asian cultures, contribute to this high percentage of Asian American non-swimmers. Because I saw Black diversity growing up, I noticed when there were no other Black kids at the pool. However, I didn't really know many other kids of Asian descent, so their absence at the pool wasn't as apparent to

---

4    Ahsan, S. (2022, November 28). Why Many South Asians Never Learn to Swim. The Juggernaut. https://www.thejuggernaut.com/why-south-asian-never-learn-to-swim

me—they were missing from most scenes in my day-to-day life growing up.

The point is that my participation in the swim team from a young age normalized the sport for me. I became comfortable in the water, and today I'm a certified scuba diver who enjoys exploring underwater ecosystems when I travel. The importance of not ascribing to cultural norms cannot be underscored enough, because so many cultural norms for people of color are prohibitive. I didn't feel out of place at the pool as a child, nor do I believe my peers saw me that way. In fact, being surrounded by kids who didn't look like me may have worked in my favor. If I had grown up with more Black or Asian friends, I might never have been introduced to swimming as a sport. To this day, I continue to swim laps weekly for exercise, something I genuinely enjoy. Yet, there's an alternate reality out there where cultural bias and exclusionary attitudes could have steered me away from the water—because, after all, as some people might say, "swimming is for white people."

## Annie

When I think back on it, I was given opportunities to be whatever I wanted to be, regardless of my skin color or ethnicity, which is truly a blessing. In eighth grade, I played the lead in our middle school production of Annie. Truth be told, I wasn't too excited to wear a frizzy red wig or to be on stage for just about every scene of the play—I had only auditioned to spend more time with my friends, and I would have been happy playing one of the chorus orphans so I could've attended rehearsals without having to memorize so many lines. The chorus teacher, however, had different plans for me. She cast me as Annie without a second thought, even though there was a sea of enthusiastic white children who would have loved to play the lead role.

The production was a success, and in the end, I was glad to have been cast in the lead. It helped strengthen my acting skills. The memorization of lines, having to conjure up a wide range of emotions on cue, singing outside of my normal vocal range, and learning to improvise when scenes didn't play out exactly as we had practiced were all skills that made me a better performer. Some of those skills have even proved useful in the workplace. Memorizing information for a presentation or thinking on my feet when things don't go as planned are skills I rely on. Playing Annie was an extremely valuable experience I never would have considered for myself. I couldn't see myself in the role, but my teacher did. Having that kind of sponsorship at such a young and impressionable age had an indelible impact on me, even if I didn't know it at the time.

Over twenty years later, when Halle Bailey—a Black woman—was cast as the lead in Disney's live-action version of *The Little Mermaid*, I was surprised and saddened by the world's reaction. While many were excited to see Bailey in this role, others were not, and they were vocal about it. Bailey was born the same year I played Annie, and when the rising young actress was cast as Ariel, it unleashed racist outrage—how dare a Black woman be cast in a traditionally white role! It's a shame that it's taking so long for diverse representation to become mainstream. How lucky I was to not have that as a barrier to my imagination in my formative years. *Mrs. Hammond, if you are reading this, thank you for believing in me.*

## Moving Out of the Spotlight

I wasn't just into acting, I was a stage kid all around. Singing was actually my first love, and I started doing so in front of audiences at age nine, but I soon crossed over into dancing and acting as well. Once I got to high school, I had a private vocal coach, and I was at the dance studio multiple nights a week after school honing my skills—mostly in character, tap, and jazz. I wanted to be famous.

I'll never forget an opportunity that came through my dance studio when I was in middle school. There was an open call for young dancers to model for a local dancewear shop's seasonal catalog. The audition required you to stand before a panel of casting directors in your nude-colored tights (which were much lighter than my skin tone) and a white leotard. This is a very revealing outfit for a young, vulnerable girl going through puberty, and auditioning took real courage. From that experience, I learned I didn't have the right body type to be a dancer, and thus I wouldn't be a good fit for the catalog. My legs were not long enough, and I wasn't thin enough. The turn-out from my hips wasn't pronounced enough. These were things I had told myself in ballet class, only now they were being voiced by grown adults with expertise in the field. This was the point at which I told myself dancing was ancillary to a singing career if I wanted to be a star. I couldn't make it as a dancer, but dancing skills might help me make it as a singer. Being a singer *and* a dancer makes you a stronger performer overall.

I sang in a variety of genres, but I really thought country music, a predominantly white genre, was my ticket to the top. In this instance, I thought standing out because of my color and my ethnicities might work in my favor. Maybe I could rise to the top by being an anomaly and become the first Black and Asian female to top the Country Billboard Chart!

Over time, I came to realize it's tough to make it as any type of performer, and I wasn't sure if I wanted stardom enough to make the sacrifices required to give it my all. So instead, I went to college for music business. It was a way to be involved in the industry and provide myself with a livable income while not having to rely on being "discovered."

Looking back, I don't believe I was truly talented enough to succeed as a full-time performer, but I do still believe that what makes me different can be used to my advantage. Standing out and being different isn't always negative. The number of women of color in the country music scene has certainly grown since I was a kid, and there is no doubt Beyoncé's recent chart-topping country album will pave the way for more. I hope to see more diversity in every genre of music, and I think the tendency for artists to fuse various sounds together to become crossover artists will help us achieve this. The blending of cultures through music is just another way of showing how the younger generations are evolving, not just in their identities, but also in how they want to be heard.

## Code-Switching

My sister has always been really good at embracing the different sides of our cultural heritages. She is a member of a historically Black sorority—one of the "Divine Nine," as they are more commonly known. She was also a member of every Asian student group on her undergraduate campus, which eventually led to her serving as president of the Asian Student Council at her college and on the national board for the Filipino Asian Student Association (FASA). She was certainly busy, and when I would visit her on campus, I found her demeanor changed slightly from group to group. There were small differences in the way she would interact with her various friend-groups, from her body language to the cultural references she would make. She never quite lost herself, but rather she seemed to be teetering between two very real identities that she just couldn't seem to blend.

I didn't know there was a term for this then, but today someone would refer to my sister's balancing acts as code-switching. Code-switching refers to the ways in which someone (consciously or unconsciously) adjusts their language, syntax, grammatical structure, behavior, and appearance to fit into a certain culture.

I like to think I consistently present myself as the same person regardless of who I'm around, but since code-switching can happen unconsciously, I can never really be sure. For example, in college, it was brought to my attention that after I would talk to friends and family from home in Virginia, I would use a heavier Southern accent. I think the reality is we all absorb and reflect certain words or tones of voice if we are exposed to them for long enough. If, for example, you visit Northern California for a while, you might start using the word *hella*, which is somewhat unique to the region. We all innately want to fit in and will adjust accordingly for it to be so.

I personally struggle with the idea of code-switching because, most often, it refers to a context where someone Black is attempting to fit into "white culture." I attended a presentation on code-switching through my employer once, during which the speaker said, "If any person of color on this call has ever been told, 'You sound like a white person,' you have performed the act of code-switching." He was wrong. The speaker made an assumption in coming to that conclusion; the assumption was that the tone of voice and vernacular used by the person of color were different from those the person used in everyday settings. I have been on the receiving end of those words, and the way I spoke to the lady who told me I "sounded white" was no different than the way I might talk to my parents or friends.

The issue with this mindset is that it assumes there is a way to "speak white" or a way to "sound Black." Depending on where a person grew up geographically, what kind of schooling they received, if accents or languages other than English were prevalent in the home, and other factors, two people of the same race could speak very differently. If a construction foreman from Brooklyn, a farmer from rural Georgia, and a tech startup founder from Silicon Valley all spoke on a panel, you might see three white males, but you would hear three distinct tones, pronunciations, cadences, etc. This is an extreme example, but the generalization that all people of the same race sound alike is also extreme. It's strange to me that when someone speaks with proper grammar in a neutral American accent (free of identifiable, regional origin) it's considered "sounding white."

With that said, the "white voice" is synonymous with professionalism, while the "Black voice" tends to be considered more casual, even street slang. As a person who grew up in a predominantly white area and attended predominantly white

institutions, the "white voice" shaped how I learned to communicate. My sister had the same experience as I did during her elementary school years, but we attended different high schools,
which is where her experience and exposure took a more diverse
path. This is where she first learned to code-switch, but in her
case, it was less about sounding professional and more about
simply fitting in with friends.

When I spoke with my sister about my reflections on this
period in her life, she expressed that, in her mind, it has never
really been about reconciling her Black and Asian roots. The
pull or tension she felt stemmed from the dichotomy of being
a minority (of any kind) in a society which inherently prioritizes whiteness. For her, it was not one side of her heritage versus
the other—it was navigating her way through a world that was
most accepting of something she so clearly was not, regardless of
which ethnicity she chose to embrace.

I think the comfort and confidence my sister has in her
identity as an adult resulted from her immersion in a variety of
cultural settings throughout her childhood and teen years. Her
going to a magnet school for government and international studies during her high school years allowed her the opportunity to
diversify her friend-groups and learn more about Asian cultures,
a luxury I didn't have. Also, her high school program was housed
inside of a predominantly Black public school (with each program occupying a different side of the building), which added
yet another layer to the diversity of her educational experience.
She took those experiences to college, where she embraced both
sides of her heritage, but it wasn't until she attended an HBCU
for medical school that my sister seemed to really find the middle

ground between her two cultural sides. Today, her comfort in her own skin is evident in the way she carries herself and in the way she approaches interactions with others in today's slightly-more-subtle yet still-very-existent culturally divided society.

It's counterintuitive, but in certain ways, getting outside of the groups you most closely associate with helps you better define who you are. It allows you to tap into your true, authentic self. My sister's exploration of associating with a variety of social groups taught me so much, even just as a spectator. For example, when I was still in high school, she invited me to her FASA events and the sorority/fraternity probates on her college campus, and I still remember how exciting and eye-opening those experiences were for me during that time. In fact, I'm sure my visits with her were what led me to explore various clubs and opportunities at NYU. As a big sister does, she was helping me find my way, and for that, I will forever be grateful.

## Safety and Representation

There are not many times in my life I can remember fearing for my safety, but there are two instances in particular that will forever live in my memory. The first was in high school. My sister drove us to an evening event at her high school in Richmond, and we were stopped by the police. I don't remember the exact reason we were pulled over, but I remember being on a narrow, dark, alley-like road when the police car turned its lights on behind us, signaling for my sister to pull over. At this particular time, the city of Richmond was not the safest place to be at night. In 1997, Richmond was named the murder capital of the

US based on its number of homicides, and I could never let that go in my mind. So, I was extremely apprehensive about pulling over, even if it was for the police. The setting of this particular street made me even more nervous.

This was before cell phones had the ability to record video, but I remember sending a text message to my then-boyfriend informing him of what was happening in case anything went wrong. My sister pulled over and rolled her window all the way down, at which point I lost it. I asked her why she felt the need to put the window *all* the way down... couldn't she just crack it? There was no one around besides the police officers, and I could see the two of them walking toward the car, one approaching on each side. I continued to text a play-by-play of what was happening to my boyfriend and tried not to fall into hysterics. What's for sure is that my heart was pounding, and I could feel tears welling up in my eyes. I was scared. We were two young girls alone at night, and we were vulnerable. I wondered if our being Black would influence the outcome of the situation, even though my sister definitely looks more Asian. As I sat there gripping my phone in my hand, my fear was overwhelming, yet somehow my sister seemed to be experiencing none of it.

After the formal back and forth that's usual for a traffic stop, the first officer wrote my sister a ticket, and we were on our way. I was in tears at this point for apparently no reason, except for the possibility of what could have gone wrong. Maybe I watched too much news, and that's why my reaction and my sister's reaction to the situation were so different? Had it been me behind the wheel, I certainly would have waited to pull over at a well-lit gas station with witnesses around.

The second fear-inducing incident happened while I was studying abroad in the Czech Republic during my junior year at NYU. All my friends were studying abroad that semester, and although I wasn't thrilled at the thought of leaving the country for four months, I caved and decided I had to go abroad too. (I must admit, this was the one time I was thankful for peer pressure.)

If I thought my hometown in Virginia lacked diversity, I hadn't seen anything yet. The center of Prague with its many tourists was speckled with minorities, but once you left the city's center, there was not a person of color in sight.

My dorm was situated in a cute little neighborhood outside the touristy part of town, and I took a tram or the subway into the city center for classes every day. One particular morning, my classmates and I were waiting for the tram when a local man walked up and began snapping photos of me. It was strange. I wasn't doing anything in particular, just sitting on the window-ledge of a shop next to the tram stop. His picture-taking wasn't really bothersome until the tram came; that's when the guy attempted to follow me as I boarded, snapping pictures the whole time. My friend was able to wave him off, but the uneasy feeling followed me around for the rest of the day.

I explained the incident to our resident assistant in the dorm, who was a local herself. She explained some of the older people in the neighborhood were not used to seeing people of different races outside of the main city, or even at all. She told me not to be alarmed, and she said I should be flattered since the man took so many photos of me. I guess that must be how celebrities feel when the paparazzi are following them around, taking photos when they're just trying to go about their daily lives. I now find the occasional backlash towards the paparazzi more understandable.

It is both a privilege and a burden to grow up in spaces where you are the only one. On the one hand, it's an opportunity to see and experience things that others who look like you may never get the chance to, and the world opens to you in a variety of ways if you are willing to become comfortable with the uncomfortable. On the other hand, you may become a token, bearing the responsibility of representing all those who look like you. It's an unspoken responsibility, but nevertheless, it's something you are always mindful of once made aware that those are the stakes at hand, and you know your behavior determines if others like you will be able to follow comfortably in your footsteps.

This tokenism plays out in a lot of ways. For instance, at an alumni event, I was talking to the associate dean of the graduate business school I attended, and she told me how another former student had expressed to her the pressure he felt as the only Black male in his cohort. He only wanted to speak in class if he felt like he was being a good representation of the Black community because anytime he spoke, he felt he was representing more than just himself. For him, every comment or question could be seen as speaking for an entire group, which is a burden his cis white classmates were probably not feeling. This constant awareness of having to "represent" made it incredibly difficult for him to speak freely or ask questions, thus inhibiting his ability to learn—a fundamental purpose of the academic classroom.

In that same fashion, I felt like my reaction to the photographer incident in the Czech Republic would have an impact on whether future students of color from NYU would want to study abroad in Prague. Letting students like me know what to expect could affect *how* they were recruited to the experience and onboarded.

The paradox I face is that in some spaces I am "Black enough" to serve as the token Black person, yet in some spaces of color, I might not even be considered Black. So, I am able to use my privilege of mixed race to open the door for others, some of whom don't feel I even represent them at all.

# PART II:

# COLLEGE INTO EARLY ADULTHOOD

Scholarships = $ FREE MONEY $

PAGEANTS as a source of learning:
- Poise
- Public Speaking
- Positive self-image

?? How much of your ?? history is documented?
- Family lineage
- Health records

Things I knew going into grad school

How much do you know about your ancestors?

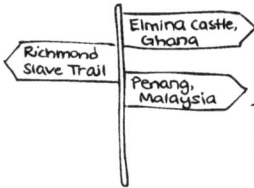

Richmond Slave Trail

Elmina castle, Ghana

Penang, Malaysia

Take time to explore your roots.

what I don't want to do | what I actually want to do

Nicknames I've had tied to race/ethnicity:
- Baby Spot
- Nyonya

CONTEXT IS KEY

Black ≃ African American

INCOGNITO
We all just want to blend in.

"No hablo español."

Provide a safe space for open conversations about hard topics.

# CHAPTER 4

# Higher Education

## *Next Stop, NYU*

WHILE MY DAD never went to college, my mom earned her nursing degree from Virginia Commonwealth University. Even with their vastly different upbringings and the two different paths they took into their careers, they both understood the value of a good education. For me and my sister, there was never a question around *if* we would go to college. The question instead was, "*Which* colleges would we attend?" By the time I was a senior in high school, my interest in (maybe you could even say "obsession with") the music industry was turning my attention to educational institutions in major cities known for their music scenes: New York City, Los Angeles, and Nashville. At that time, there were very few schools offering a program specifically designed around the business of the music industry. So, seeking out such a niche program really narrowed down my options.

To please my parents, I applied to a handful of schools in Virginia as well. I knew attending an in-state school would be significantly cheaper than attending a school out of state, but I was hoping for a drastic change of scenery. I wanted to experience something new and move to a place where no one knew me. College would be a chance to reinvent myself and step into adulthood. When you grow up in a small town, you are forever tied to the identity formed by the actions of your youth. In my mind, it was only possible to shed that immature identity by going somewhere far away where my past would not follow me—to an institution large enough that, even if someone from my childhood was enrolled there, I would have the space to blossom into my full potential, without inhibitions.

Most kids from my graduating class, if they chose to pursue higher education, went to an in-state college, and Virginia has many great colleges and universities to choose from. I, however, had my sights set on NYU. In 2004, NYU topped *The Princeton Review*'s "dream college" rankings, beating even Harvard University for the first-place spot.[5] High school students at the time were enamored with schools in urban areas where they could connect with the larger world via in-class and out-of-class experiences. I agreed with the masses because I understood proximity to the music industry also meant proximity to internships and job opportunities. NYU offered a Bachelor of Music in music business, and so despite the high private-school price tag, I was very interested in the program. If I somehow managed to get into this highly competitive program, I knew there was no way my parents would agree to let me attend without financial assistance. And so, the journey began to not only impress the admissions committee, but also to figure out how much money I had already accrued for my college education and how much

---

5   The Crimson. (2004, March 18). NYU tops new dream rankings. Retrieved from https://www.thecrimson.com/article/2004/3/18/nyu-tops-new-dream-rankings-the/

more I would need to make a persuasive argument for the college of my dreams.

## *The Importance of Documentation*

Paying for college can be a game of strategy if you know what you're doing. There's no denying college is expensive, but there is also a lot of free money in the form of scholarships for students who are willing to do the research and put in the work. My mom (and, later on, my sister) were professionals at this. They assisted me in fielding the scholarship system to maximize the financial aid that would help put me through my undergraduate program. Under my mom's guidance, I started entering essay contests and scholarship pageants when I was in elementary school to save up for the inevitable college-tuition bill.

Yes, I did say scholarship pageants. There are beauty pageants that give college scholarships as prizes. I entered into a handful of these scholarship pageants during my elementary through high school years. The pageant circuit taught me poise and public speaking. It helped me build my confidence and my resume. It taught me how to present my best self in an interview. Scholarship pageantry placed importance on not just looking your best, but on giving your best to your schoolwork and to your community. I credit much of my positive self-image to my participation in the Little Future Miss of Virginia pageant at age nine. It was a surprisingly diverse and inclusive environment where I felt seen, heard, and valued. While pageants might not be the right fit for all children, every young person should have some sort of experience that's both diverse and inclusive.

Most of the other scholarship money I received came through application processes where I needed to submit a record of my accomplishments—academic and otherwise—and some required writing an essay in response to a given prompt. Many scholarships were restricted to students who lived in a specific area, came from households with a specific income level, or were of a specific ethnicity.

I was able to apply to scholarships for African Americans and Asian Americans, but one set of scholarships I was not able to take advantage of were those offered to people of Native American heritage. I know my father's family has some Native American roots, but I have no paperwork to prove it. Our family is not currently registered with any tribe, and while my dad's sister has tried to locate records to prove our lineage and educate us on our past, she hasn't had much luck.

Written records are not abundant on either side of my family. I was fortunate to be able to meet the documentation requirements for many scholarships for people of color, but those documents only go back a generation or two. Even if you were to try to trace back my African American roots, you would only get so far. The documenting of African Americans in American history often boils down to the bills of sale of enslaved persons. To complicate matters, bills of sale were only necessary if money was exchanged, so not all transactions of human beings were documented. For instance, if an enslaved person was given as a gift or traded for goods or services, there may not be documentation. On top of that, not all births and deaths of the enslaved were documented, either. So there are many holes in our history.

On my mother's side of the family, I don't know too many details about our lineage, but I do know my mom's mom didn't have her original birth certificate. The birth certificate she used as official documentation actually belonged to one of her siblings who died young, we believe. We only estimated her age based on anecdotal stories from her childhood.

There are health issues abounding on both sides of my family that I would like to sit and document for the sake of my own lineage, should I ever have children. Both my dad's and my mom's families have passed this information down verbally, but like in a game of telephone, the facts become distorted over time, as our memories are not always reliable and accurate.

History books are also not effective at telling the diverse stories of America's history. It was not until my adult years that I realized there were *zero* Asian American history lessons taught throughout my schooling. In the US, we always hear people talk about how suppressed and distorted African American history is, and that certainly needs to be addressed, but there are so many more forgotten groups of people who made great contributions to this country and the freedoms and privileges we enjoy today. They also deserve pages in our history books.

History will not write itself, so it's up to us to document what we know. With advances in technology, this shouldn't be a difficult task. There are voice-to-text programs that allow you to simply record an oral history, and the program will convert your speech to written text. You can then feed that written text into any number of artificial intelligence tools that can clean up the grammar and/or edit the writing to fit the style of documentation you wish to create. There are also products like Storyworth, which preserve meaningful moments and memories for generations to come by prompting the storytelling process slowly over time, making it seem more manageable.

We live in the age of information, where data is being collected to capitalize on our every interest and desire through targeted marketing, but we certainly aren't applying this technology to capture all the information that really matters at the same scale. Future generations will know all the trends we created—what we wore, what memes were popular—but not necessarily who we were or the values that we built our lives around. It is up to us to flood the historical records with the information we are proud of and want to be remembered for, and it is up to us to document the information that future generations can learn and grow from.

My journey of applying to college taught me more than just how to navigate the complex world of scholarships—it underscored the critical importance of documentation in shaping one's future. From compiling records of academic achievement to writing essays that showcased my unique story, I learned how essential it is to have a well-documented history. This experience instilled in me a deeper appreciation for the power of preserving family stories and cultural history, not just for my own benefit, but for the benefit of generations that follow.

## Continuing My Education

The idea of going to graduate business school was always something I had tucked away in the back of my mind. It seemed like a logical step in progressing towards success, but I didn't attach a timeline of any sort to it. I just thought, "Maybe I'll go back for a graduate degree someday." That "someday" came when I returned home from living abroad in Malaysia with no plan for what to do next. With no job lined up upon my return, it seemed like the perfect time to advance my studies.

With almost five years of work experience under my belt, I knew more about what I *didn't* want to do than what I *did* want to do with my career. That knowledge still proved valuable as I considered programs to apply to, paying special attention to the coursework they offered as well as the opportunities available in each university's city. Just as when I was applying to undergraduate programs, I wanted to be able to take advantage of out-of-class experiences in addition to my in-class experiences. I also wanted to try out a new city, some place I hadn't spent much time in but was intrigued by.

A friend from NYU had gone on to pursue her master's in business administration (MBA) from the University of North Carolina at Chapel Hill, and so I reached out to see what I could learn from her. What she shared was so much more than just her experience in grad school. She pointed me to a network of professionals who not only graduated from the nation's top business schools, but who also looked like me. This network would help me determine where to apply to school and set me up for success once I was admitted.

## *The Consortium for Graduate Study in Management*

The MBA network my friend connected me with is referred to as The Consortium. This organization aims to break the glass ceiling by offering African Americans, Hispanic Americans, and Native Americans opportunities to attend the nation's top MBA programs. By creating a diverse pipeline into these educational institutions and partnering with major corporations, The Consortium opens doors for underrepresented students to reach executive positions. I was fortunate enough to receive one of their full-tuition fellowships for my MBA.

As I was preparing to enter graduate school at the University of Texas, The Consortium brought together students from across the nation along with all their member schools for one big MBA orientation. Then, during the summer prior to that first semester, I was even paired with a Consortium buddy in my same class year so I would already have a friend going into my first day on campus. In the days leading up to my first day of grad school, my university had additional orientation events for Consortium students. I appreciate the efforts that were made to ensure Consortium members felt comfortable on our campuses and in our new university communities.

The Consortium continues to support its graduates even beyond their MBA programs for those who choose to engage. Job postings as well as educational and networking opportunities are communicated through the alumni network. They even have their own networking and social engagement platform called Hello Fellow. I graduated from the McCombs School of Business at The University of Texas, where the Consortium alumni specific to our school have an engaged network. Each fall, as part of the University of Texas's alumni homecoming weekend, the Consortium Family hosts a brunch to gather those who have come back to campus so they can reminisce and reconnect. There are ways to get involved with the organization on the national level too, but each school has their own ways of keeping their network active.

As an additional effort to reach forward and pull up the next generation, I have more recently gotten involved with the newly established McCombs Black Alumni Association. The association was founded when a small group of more-recent graduates banded together to try to recruit more students of color into the University of Texas's MBA program. I volunteer on a committee working to create scholarship opportunities for these prospective students.

To whom much is given, much is required. So, when I was asked to speak about my MBA experience at the second annual McCombs Black Alumni Association Gala, I happily accepted the invitation. This was my chance to help rally our fellow alumni to create opportunities for future Black MBA students who might not be considering our program and who would thus miss out on the amazing opportunities that have led graduates like me to where we are today. For those of us who have had excellent educational and professional opportunities, it's our responsibility to ensure the next generation is equally (if not increasingly) blessed.

My time at McCombs connected me to SXSW (South by Southwest), an annual conference and festival at the convergence of music, film, technology, and culture. It also afforded me the opportunity to study abroad for a semester in Tokyo, Japan. It connected me to folks who have gone on to lead amazing careers at iconic companies such as Coca-Cola, Starbucks, Apple, and Google.

Those contacts have been invaluable as I've navigated my own career, and they came in especially handy when curating guest speakers during my time as an adjunct professor at Virginia Commonwealth University's da Vinci Center for Innovation. Through my graduate school network, I've discovered true professional growth comes not just from advancing personally, but from lifting others to come alongside me. Each connection made, each opportunity shared, becomes a stepping stone for future generations of diverse business leaders.

# CHAPTER 5

# Cultural Heritage on Campus

*You'll Never Be…*

One thing you see a lot in New York City is ethnic pride. The city is home to the Puerto Rican Day Parade and the Brooklyn West Indian Carnival, among many, many other ethnic festivals, both large and small. There are neighborhoods throughout the various boroughs where the cultures of other countries thrive. These neighborhoods and celebrations give people who identify with their associated ethnic groups spaces and places to embrace their heritage as well as one another.

As a combination of various ethnicities, I don't really associate myself with one culture over the other, even though it always felt to me as if American culture wanted me to choose. I love that people embrace their cultural heritages and take pride in where their ancestors came from. However, I do find it hard to participate in any of these celebrations as more than an interested outsider.

Growing up, my closest friends were mostly Caucasian. I come from a predominantly white town, so that's not really surprising. But Black students had a presence too, and I noticed they mostly hung out with each other. They ate lunch together and attended sporting events together. In my mind, there was a bond they all shared that I could never be a part of. We were certainly friendly whenever we passed each other in the halls, but I was not in their circle. I'm not sure what created it, but there was always a clear racial divide in the classrooms, cafeteria, and even within sports teams. Everyone seemed to get along, but for some reason or another, kids always gravitated to other kids who looked like them. As I grew older, I tried to make friends with all the various cliques—white and Black alike—but that never seemed to help break down racial lines any further. It just meant more friendly waves as I walked through the halls.

It has occurred to me in more recent years that those divides were likely in large part due to geographic and familial ties. Maybe students weren't just gravitating to people who looked like themselves, but rather to those who lived near them and rode the bus with them. Perhaps they felt more comfortable around the kids of their parents' friends. What I was seeing as a young person were the after-effects of generational segregation in the rural South, and I was just too young to understand it all. And I certainly wasn't taught academically to think in that manner.

When I was at NYU, I attempted to embrace various cultural groups. I joined the NAACP on campus, which was a very active association. I attended meetings and served on a couple of event boards when I could find the time. It was a great way to meet people and make friends. NAACP members were always welcoming and inclusive toward me, and I felt relieved by this. Sometimes, I would see some of the NAACP members hanging out together in my dorm, and it soon became clear to me that even in a city as diverse as New York, people still gravitated toward people who looked like them.

I later joined the International Filipino Association's dance team. I had a couple of friends already on the team, and I just wanted to dance. (Before I joined, I was a member of NYU's official competition dance team during my freshman and sophomore years.) Although I'm not at all Filipino, there were no Malaysian clubs on campus, and there was certainly no Malaysian dance team, so I joined the Asian club that most appealed to my interests. No one in the club ever made me feel as though I wasn't "Filipino enough" to dance with them. In fact, everyone was very welcoming. Nonetheless, it's hard to assimilate into a cultural group when you don't know anything about the culture in question. I had never been to the Philippines and wasn't familiar with their traditions, which did sometimes play into our routines. That had an odd effect on me. Instead of hearing others saying I wasn't "enough" for the group, I found my own mind beginning to self-criticize, asking why I chose to put myself into a place where I didn't belong.

Something that was making others feel so comforted—i.e., the full embrace of culture and being around others who shared that culture—had the opposite effect on me. It made me feel uncomfortable. The lack of peers who shared a mixed background like mine sometimes felt isolating. We all just want to feel like we belong, especially during childhood, but also as young adults and all throughout our lives.

## Baby Spot

Nicknames can often be thought of as terms of endearment. I have had many nicknames throughout my life, but in college there was one in particular that taught me a lot about the importance of context and communication. Not everything is always as it seems.

They told me college would be a big transition, but I didn't really believe them. "They" were my parents, teachers, and any adult in my life, but I had been to sleepaway camp for multiple summers growing up—I knew what it was to bunk with strangers who would become friends. I was excited at the prospect of being a small-town country girl in the big city. NYU is at the center of all the metropolitan action, and I couldn't wait to get there. From my perspective, the question wasn't, "Am I ready for New York City?" Rather, the question was, "Is New York City ready for *me*?"

As had happened many times before, "they" were right. The city was overwhelming, and so was college life. I had never been surrounded by so many people while still feeling so alone. The first few weeks of classes revealed exactly how unprepared I was. Despite having good grades throughout high school, I had never truly learned how to study—and at a school like NYU, you *need* good study techniques and habits. I made friends with the girls in my dorm, but when my roommate and I stopped getting along well, all the girls from the dorm chose to hang out with her instead of me. I went from having many new friends to feeling like I had no friends at all pretty quickly.

Luckily, this was around the time the dance team's try-outs were beginning. I had always wanted to be on a dance team. So much so that, in my junior year of high school, I had attempted to start a team within our athletic department. It never took off, though—despite my having found a faculty sponsor, the administration claimed there was no space for us to practice after school. So I settled for choreographing the dance portions of our competition cheerleading routines as I anxiously awaited my opportunity to try out for a dance team at the collegiate level. When I got to college, NYU not only had a dance team, but their team was ranked among the top that competed in the National Dance Alliance's Collegiate Championship every year in Daytona Beach, Florida, so I was eager to gain a spot.

I gave try-outs my all, and thankfully it was enough to land me among the four freshmen to make the team. We were welcomed onto the team with an initiation party in one of the upperclassmen's dorms, and it was there I learned I had been given the nickname Baby Spot. In my mind, having a nickname made me even more a part of the group, and at that point in my very short tenure as a college student, I was just excited to have new friends in a big city that felt very isolating. I didn't give any thought to the nickname itself or what it meant.

It wasn't until years later when someone asked me about the nickname, which was embroidered across the top flap of my travel-team duffel-bag, that I really thought about how I got the nickname. Prior to my joining the team, there was only one Black dancer, and her nickname was Spot. I was told she'd been given that name because—when you're sitting at a distance in the stands watching the team perform—she was the obvious "spot" dancing among the group, as her skin color made her stand out. During try-outs, I was one of the few Black girls auditioning. (In fact, I may have been the only Black girl trying out... it's hard to recall now after so many years.) As a younger and more petite Black dancer, it seemed obvious to the more senior girls on the team that my nickname would be Baby Spot.

Especially as a freshman, I embraced my new nickname fully without question, and I never felt othered by it. Through my years at NYU—and even for years after I graduated—I traveled with that duffel bag proudly showcasing I was a dance team member. I never once stopped to consider I was also showing off a nickname that labeled me as a token Black girl. When I reflect on my experience with the dance team, in no way do I feel I was chosen for the team because I was Black, nor do I feel my skin color made me closer to the one other Black girl on the team. However, I do find it strange that it took me nearly a decade to really give all this much thought, and when I did, I immediately felt embarrassed by it. I got rid of the duffel bag and, until now, I never spoke of it again.

The nickname was supposed to be a term of endearment. Paradoxically, a nickname which called me out as being different from most of the other girls was the very thing that made me feel more included as a part of the group. It makes me wonder how many other things I overlooked in the name of peer acceptance throughout the course of my younger years. But things aren't always what they seem, and I later discovered that the origins of that nickname were not exactly what I had imagined.

I have stayed in touch with Spot over the years, and it was only recently that she revealed to me the actual story of how those nicknames came to be. In her freshman year on the dance team, team members regularly watched video playbacks for review after each performance. The videos were fuzzy, low-quality VHS tapes, which made it impossible to recognize individual team members. The team members would constantly be asking "Who's that?" as they reviewed the footage, but Spot always knew which dancer was her. There was a dark-skinned Filipino girl on the team who was the only member who took to calling her Spot, and that was only after Spot herself had called attention to her obviously being the dark "spot" moving across the screen. Spot then gave me the nickname Baby Spot, which somehow was fully adopted by the entire team. But of course, it was in the spirit of inclusivity, despite how it might sound now.

When revealing the true origin of the nickname to me, I could tell how embarrassed Spot was. I could sense in her the same reaction as I'd had in the moment of clarity that led me to my tossing out my embroidered duffel bag. Yet we had both lived through it all with nothing but love for one another and for the team as a whole. This story just proves that sometimes what is seemingly racist may not be what you think. The rooted racism in this country runs deep, and it flares emotions often, but it's also important for us to assume good intentions and communicate with others. Context is key, and without conversation, you might be lacking that context.

## Black Does Not Mean African American

Growing up in a place where people are regarded as colors and not ethnicities, I learned to use the words *Black* and *African American* interchangeably. What I didn't realize is not all Black people in America identify as African American. Not all Black people in America think of their heritage as African, largely because their families came to this country by way of somewhere else. Often that "somewhere else" is a country in the Caribbean, like Jamaica or the Dominican Republic. While some may argue these populations all got to their current locations by way of Africa somewhere in the historical timeline, African American is still not an identity all Black people in the US want to or will identify with.

The baggage that comes with being African American is heavy. The impact the slave trade had on American culture and commerce is, at an understatement, messy and traumatic. I can understand why someone would choose not to identify with the past if they can't directly tie themselves to it. And not wanting to be connected to the horrors of America's racial past might not even be the reason some have for not claiming the African American identity. Some may just have a very strong affinity for their homeland, or for the homeland of their parents or grandparents. (And, for descendants of immigrants from such countries, whatever that homeland may be, it's likely a place they have traveled to and a culture with which they have firsthand experience.) Conversely, many African Americans have never even thought about visiting one of the thousands of beautiful locations in Africa, but they know that's where their ancestors came from. They proudly claim that heritage today as the descendants of people who endured great hardship and still managed to survive.

While I'm pretty positive my Black roots tie directly back to Africa, I still bring this up because it's something I had never thought about until I met Black people in New York City who didn't identify as African American. I also think it's an interesting example of how we tend to generalize large groups of people in America. We simply see with our eyes, and we impose ideas about who that person is and what background they come from without asking any questions.

# CHAPTER 6

# Scholars Trips and Other Global Experiences

## *Walking with My Ancestors*

THERE IS SOMETHING about experiencing a place, a specific geographic location, that cannot be replicated, even with the help of recent advancements in technology. Sure, you can visit somewhere using augmented reality or virtual reality, and those tools will closely simulate the experience of being somewhere you are not, but to feel the spirits of the ancestors in the air, along with the stories untold in the ground under your feet, requires physically standing in that place.

I have traveled to the lands of the ancestors on both sides of my family, and that's how I know this. As an adult now living in Richmond, I'm right in the heart of where the American slave trade once flourished. After the transatlantic slave trade was abolished in the early 1800s, which ended the importation of enslaved people into the US but did nothing about the domestic slave trade, Richmond became the second-largest slave market on the East Coast. It became a major hub for selling enslaved Black Virginians and other people of African descent down into the Deep South. It's a dark and complicated history, which is why in 2011 the Richmond Slave Trail was established. It's a two-and-a-half-mile trail that goes from the historic Manchester Docks, where large ships would unload hundreds of people onto the muddy, tree-lined banks of the James River, across a bridge over rocky rapids, and into the city center's old slave auction houses in Shockoe Bottom. On this trail, you hike over the exact steps of enslaved people would have walked in chains in the 1700s and 1800s.

My first experience with feeling the emotional weight of the slave trade took place 5,000 miles from my history-laden home. In 2006, on a scholars' trip to Ghana during my sophomore year of undergrad, I visited Elmina Castle, one of the principal slave depots of the transatlantic slave trade for more than three centuries. The stories of "happy slaves" that were taught to me in grade school were immediately corrected and replaced with truths of a dark past. Walking through the Door of No Return—a narrow passageway in Elmina Castle that led enslaved Africans out to the vast Atlantic Ocean where slave ships awaited—and contemplating all the suffering the enslaved endured before even making it to the plantations of the Americas had a profound effect on me. The initial march of enslaved persons to Elmina Castle could have taken anywhere from several days to several weeks. Then came additional weeks or even months held in the castle in captivity; this was prior to the short march that preceded the six- to twelve-week journey aboard a ship while confined under horrific conditions.

My paternal grandparents' house was in a county full of plantations where the enslaved once worked and lived, and this wasn't something I'd really dedicated any thought to until I made the trip to Ghana. Having that realization as the starting point on my quest for a more robust telling of my ancestors' journey made walking the Richmond Slave Trail an even more powerful experience. Even though the trail was established in 2011, it wasn't until 2016 that I could bring myself to walk past every historical marker end-to-end. There is something both humbling and liberating about visiting these places and feeling the pain of our past juxtaposed with the comfort of our present lifestyle and the promise of an even greater future.

In a similar way, when I visited Penang, Malaysia with my mom, I felt a sense of awakening to the truths of a much more recent line in my family genealogy. My mom grew up in a house with many aunts, uncles, and cousins, so I had always envisioned the home to be rather large; I discovered something much different when we arrived at her old home on Victoria Street. Since the house is no longer in the family, we didn't knock or try to go in, but we did walk around the outside of the property. Mom was able to show me the old bathroom, which was simply the sewer waterway that ran behind the house. It put so much more context around the few stories she had told me about her childhood. I'm thankful to have had that experience.

Immersing myself in the places where each side of my family originated brought my ancestors' stories to life and helped solidify the foundations of my own identity. What I have seen with my own eyes far outweighs anything I could ever read in books. While I realize not everyone will have the opportunity to examine their heritage in this way, there are other means through which the rich history of our various peoples and groups can be explored.

In catering to the masses, schools will never be able to help all children understand the roots from which they come. For many reasons, so many lessons in school only teach a single, incomplete perspective of history; it's very important for us all to seek out supplemental teachings that show a variety of perspectives, all of which have shaped the world we live in today.

## Nyonya

In my early twenties, I had what I refer to as an "*Eat, Pray, Love*" moment (i.e., a personal journey of self-discovery, though not one necessarily as extravagant as the one depicted in Elizabeth Gilbert's memoir) when I moved to Malaysia to find myself. I used to think "finding yourself" was a silly phrase, but having had the experience, I get it now. When you remove yourself from everything and everyone that's familiar to you, you realize what is really important. What do you actually miss? What do you truly need to be happy?

Since I would be living in Malaysia for quite some time, I took a job bartending at a resort on an island called Sibu in the South China Sea. Sibu is a thirty-minute boat ride off the southeast coast of the Malaysian peninsula, and when I arrived there, it was stunning. The island is in the middle of a protected marine park, so its coral reef is colorful and thriving with sea life. It was here that I became certified in scuba diving.

The resort was small, with only twenty chalets (guest rooms) for rent. The entire front-of-house staff were foreigners, while all the back-of-house staff were locals. I was the only American on staff. Most others came from the UK, with the exception of one Canadian. There were only seven of us total in the front of the house, and one of the scuba diving instructors also served as the manager for the back-of-house staff. He was both foreign and local, as his dad grew up in Malaysia, but his mom was from the UK. He split his time between the two places growing up, so he spoke both English and Malay fluently.

Although the back-of-house manager and I were both of blended backgrounds, I didn't have his ability to toggle between the two languages. I only speak English, and I hadn't spent any time in Malaysia prior to my arrival. There was certainly an adjustment period for the first few weeks, which I think was less about Malaysian culture and more about island life, and there was certainly a language barrier to field with some of the local staff.

The chalets where the foreign staff slept were the chalets not quite fit for resort guests. Perhaps we didn't have mosquito nets, or maybe there was no hot water in our rooms. My chalet fit both those descriptions, so to deal with the shower situation, I learned to wake up early and go for a run—that way I would be hot and sweaty before hopping into the cold shower. To manage the lack of netting, I lit mosquito coils next to my bed every night and hoped that would be enough to keep the bugs away. My accommodations felt more like a rustic sleepaway camp than a resort, but I adjusted and learned to love life there.

One of my favorite parts of working at the resort was the food. Rarely would we get to eat the fancy meals served to the guests. Instead, we ate local cuisine that was less dependent on the delivery schedule from the mainland. This meant a lot of fish. This also meant a lot of spice. I had loved spicy foods as a kid, but by the time I was in my twenties, my body became less able to handle the heat. The way to curb heavy spice in a Malaysian meal is to add an egg. This helps to mellow out the heat, especially if you don't cook the yolk all the way through and mix it into the dish thoroughly. So, as you can imagine, I ate many runny eggs during my time at the resort. The chef always laughed about my intolerance for spice.

The chef and I formed a friendship partly because I wanted to learn all I could while I was there. Sometimes I would help in the kitchen if I wasn't needed at the bar—that way, I could try to learn a few things to take home with me. The chef gave me the nickname Nyonya, which was a term I wasn't familiar with. Having a nickname made me feel less like a foreigner and more like a local, especially as it was given to me by one of the back-of-house staff members. To be acknowledged by someone on the island as being Malay was both surprising and deeply affirming, as it—at first—gave me a sense of belonging that I hadn't expected.

I later learned the term *nyonya* is the Malay word for a woman who is both Chinese and Malay. I had thought what would make me stand out while I was working in Malaysia was my being an American, and for some people I met, that was true. For others, what stood out was that my Malaysian roots were not pure Malay, but instead Chinese-Malay. I was simply thought of as a *nyonya*.

Through my travels, I have learned racism and colorism exist everywhere. In Malaysia, you will find that the locals of Chinese and Indian descent are treated differently than those of full Malaysian heritage. This is why my mom never had the desire to take my sister and me to Malaysia—she was unsure of how we would be treated. My mom might not be biracial, but she is certainly multiethnic. China and Malaysia are different culturally, and when she was growing up, she saw the differences in how people were treated based on their ethnic origins—and sometimes, based just on their appearances.

Skin color in many Asian cultures is viewed by some as an indicator of socioeconomic status. Dark skin equates to outdoor manual labor, thus a lower status. Skin the color of porcelain is the ideal. Because so many Asian skincare products contain skin-lightening chemicals, I had to pack enough skincare products to get me through my time on the island or be prepared to ask loved ones to ship me the products I needed. Colorism has long been a problem in America (even within Black communities), but it's important to recognize these issues extend well beyond American soil.

In America, the tides of colorism are turning. Looking around, I see more and more interracial relationships and multiracial children. Within just a few generations, there will be more racially ambiguous Americans than there will be those who are easily categorized into one box or the other. I wonder what other parts of the world are also feeling this shift.

## *Saying Goodbye*

I truly believe everything happens for a reason. While I was in Malaysia, my great aunt passed away not long before I was scheduled to meet and visit family with my mom and sister. My great aunt was my grandma's sister, who helped raise my mom and was one of the people I was most excited to meet. I was devastated that she passed just before I got the chance to meet her, but what resulted from her passing was the opportunity for me to meet much more of my extended family as they came together in this time of loss. What also resulted from my great aunt's death was the opportunity for us to attend her funerary services. I had never been to a funeral outside of the US before, and I'd never been to one that followed traditions of a non-American culture.

This was such a mind-opening experience. While my mom's extended family lives in Malaysia, they adhere to many traditions of Chinese culture. One such tradition is the wake, where the body of the deceased is placed in an open casket in the family home for viewing. For three days after the passing, loved ones are welcome to come pay their respects. There are chants made as part of the final goodbyes, and while I didn't take part in the recitations for lack of know-how, I did participate in the circling of the body and the burning of the joss sticks. (Joss sticks are long, slender incense sticks with a gentle scent that lingers in the air, creating a calming atmosphere. In many Asian traditions, they are commonly used in spiritual rituals, meditation, and cultural ceremonies). The wake was a jarring experience at first, because the woman to whom we were paying our respects was someone I had never met, and because as I looked over into the casket, I saw that my great aunt was the spitting image of my grandma. On the one hand, it was startling, but on the other, it helped bridge the gap for me and made me feel a bit less like an outsider.

This was the first time I had been to a family funeral where not only did I not know the deceased, but I also didn't know most of those in attendance. Of course, there were family members I had met prior to arriving at the house, but that had been only a few days before. It was just my mom and my sister in my circle of comfort, and the three of us were navigating these waters together. My mom hadn't seen most of these family members in decades, and she was long out of practice in speaking the language. So, we did the best we could to interact with the rest of the family, with my sister and me balancing respectful conversation around the events at hand, meeting family members for the first time, and getting to know one another. In my mom's case, she spent the time reuniting with her people and catching up on forty years of major life events.

After the third day of viewing at the family home, there is a procession to move the body to a funeral parlor. The family walks behind the hearse as the body is relocated, and everyone wears white. This is the opposite of what I'd become accustomed to in the States, where black is the usual and expected dress at funerals.

I met aunts, uncles, and cousins, some of whom spoke English and some of whom did not, but thankfully there was always someone around to help translate. It was interesting to me to start putting the family tree together in my head, making the associations that explained how I was related to each person, and figuring out how they were related to each other. When I was with my dad's family at home, the family tree was something I just innately knew and understood. In contrast, my connections to my Malaysian family—and their connections to each other— required active sorting in my mind as I moved from conversation to conversation. As is customary at Chinese funerals, family members wore armbands of different colors signifying their relationship to the deceased, which helped reinforce learning for me as I tried to piece together the family tree.

While on this trip, we also went to visit the grave of my mom's dad, who died when she was only three. While I couldn't read the Chinese characters on his grave marker, there was an image of him imposed upon the headstone—in his face, I could clearly see some of my mom's features. We again paid our respects by burning joss sticks, a tradition I would liken to leaving flowers at someone's gravesite here in the States.

We also visited my great-grandparents' ashes, which are in urns placed in Penang's Reclining Buddha temple. My mom calls the temple the Sleeping Buddha, which is how the locals refer to it. The Reclining Buddha is thirty-three meters in length, making it one of the largest Buddha statues in the world. To think I have ancestors buried in such a well-known temple gives me a certain sense of pride, almost as if it legitimizes my Asian ancestry somehow. While this may not hold any real significance—a spot in the temple is obtained through payment, much like purchasing a plot in a cemetery—the profound presence of the Buddha lends a sense of reverence and elevates the experience of being among the departed.

While I have been to many funerals in the US, I cannot say they have all been alike. The differences stem from a number of things, largely religion or family tradition, but these differences can usually also be tied to the cultural roots of the deceased. On my dad's side of the family, many funerals have been referred to as home-going services. This is a religious reference that means the deceased has "gone home" to be with the Lord. It is rooted in the Southern African American Christian tradition, something I didn't really think about until I attended a funeral with my husband, as he had never been to services of this nature.

When my dad's brother, my uncle, passed, there was a short wake just prior to the funeral service, where attendees were invited to the front of the funeral home to view the body. I have seen wakes held a day in advance of the funeral service as well, which fully separates the two events. After the viewing, there was a procession for the family to enter the main hall of the funeral home before the start of the service. The service itself included the singing of hymns, a eulogy to reflect on the life of the deceased, an open-invite period for attendees to share their fond memories, and even a short sermon to ensure the focus is less on the loss of a life here on Earth and more on the addition of a new soul in heaven.

After the service for my uncle at the funeral home, a procession of cars then followed the hearse to the gravesite where my uncle was to be laid in his final resting place. The graveside service is a much shorter service, and sometimes mourners choose to attend the funeral-home service *or* the graveside service instead of going to both. My uncle was laid to rest in the cemetery next to the church he attended his entire life, his plot next to other family members.

I have been to funerals that are referred to as celebrations of life. Often the body is not present but has already been cremated. The service is more of a casual gathering for family and friends to reminisce about good times. It isn't religious in nature, but it is an opportunity to simply celebrate the privilege of having known the deceased, and it's possibly even a time to pledge to keep the deceased's memory alive.

There are so many ways to say final goodbyes, and they are all beautiful in their own way. Death is a harsh reality that we all process differently when it casts its dark shadow in our lives, and I feel fortunate to have witnessed a variety of ways to pay respects to those who have passed on from this life before me. Having experienced the events that follow a loved one's death multiple times now, I have come to realize that, while it is important for me to get my affairs in order so my own death will not be a huge logistical burden on the people I leave behind, the way in which my life will be celebrated will be less about me and more about what will bring comfort to my loved ones. I obviously won't be alive to take part in the funeral, so I hope that whatever service is held for me will be reminiscent of the spirit I carried throughout my life, while also being comforting to those in attendance. That might be a traditional service or an event some may find to be a bit more unconventional, but I'm sure I will smile down on those who pay their respects either way; I'll just be grateful my life made an impact.

I think it will be interesting to see how death is handled as the world as a whole evolves. Land is a finite resource, so traditional burials will not be a viable option forever. Today, some people choose to forego burials and donate their bodies to science, while for others, there are companies that have found more innovative, eco-friendly ways to treat human remains. I know of one company which uses cremated remains for reef rehabilitation under the sea. I have heard of another which sells mushroom coffins; the fungi remove toxins and heavy metals from the body before returning it to nature.

When I think about how those I leave behind will handle my remains and celebrate my life, I don't really think much about how they will decide between the various cultural traditions of our family. Instead, I think more about how society is evolving and the world is changing. In this instance, it seems that ethnicity matters less: It's seemingly inevitable that, as time goes on, what makes us all the same (in this case, death) will bring us closer together around universal traditions that transcend ethnic and racial lines.

## Feeling Incognito

In my late twenties, while on a flight from Japan to Thailand, I sat next to a stranger. This gentleman began speaking to me in Thai, but he then immediately recognized I wasn't comprehending his words. He switched to English and asked, "Are you not Thai?" I was fully flattered by his assumption, as I hadn't done much traveling in that particular part of Southeast Asia and was excited at the prospect of going to a foreign country where I might blend in nicely with the local crowd.

Excited as I was, this encounter actually encouraged me to speak *less* for the remainder of the trip. I thought that, maybe, if I didn't speak, I might be mistaken for a local. I viewed this as a positive, as it probably meant a lesser chance of getting swindled by tourist traps and inflated pricing.

Sometimes this was a sound tactic, as you can move through the world more seamlessly than I'd realized without using speech. There are ways to communicate through simple facial expressions or basic body language, like a small nod of appreciation, which can take you pretty far. The problems I encountered mostly stemmed from not being able to translate what I was hearing rather than needing to give a verbal response. For instance, when I was paying for purchases, I simply had to trust I was being given the correct change, as I usually wasn't really sure how much I was being charged and was also sometimes guessing at which bills and coins to give the cashier. Sometimes I just had to hope the money I handed over would be enough.

I'm a very verbal communicator by nature. I use words not just to convey meaning, but sometimes also as a way of filling the air. As I get older, I'm becoming more comfortable with silence, but in my younger years, I never let the air go silent for long enough that I might learn to appreciate it. One of the great lessons I've learned over the years is that you can hear a lot in the silence. You start to pay more attention to things you might normally overlook, allowing you in some ways to better understand the people around you. If you aren't speaking or thinking about what you will say next, you're able to more actively listen and experience the moment. You might pick up on tension between other people in the room or notice norms in behavior among others that you are not accustomed to or were not even aware of.

While the silence on my Thailand trip was a good exercise in listening more and talking less, it was also an exercise in how it feels to move through the world incognito—maybe not necessarily in disguise, but in such a way that you don't stand out. Not standing out is often a goal of mine, and sometimes I wonder what it feels like to truly blend into an environment, because even when those around me are not noticing my otherness, I often am.

I didn't realize this feeling is normal until I saw my husband, a white male, in an environment where he felt incognito. For our honeymoon, we traveled to Scotland, a place where he has extended family and ancestral roots but that he had never been to before. Scotland is not a terribly diverse country, so most people looked like him. The ease with which he approached every activity on the trip felt very different from our day-to-day life in a gentrifying neighborhood in Richmond. Of course, this was our honeymoon, and I should've expected that we would both move with such lightness. But then I saw the same lightness in him appear again when we traveled to visit a friend in a rural, non-diverse area of Vermont. I brought it up to him when we returned home, and through that conversation, I learned he is constantly aware of his surroundings and contemplating how he might be viewed by others. There is a stress that arises from feeling as though you don't quite belong. Whether you do or don't fit in is actually irrelevant. What matters to your stress level is if *you* feel otherness is radiating off you for people to observe and judge.

Ways of not fitting in seem infinite. The gentleman on the airplane asked me, "Are you not Thai?" simply because I didn't understand the language. But language alone doesn't determine belonging; within a single country, speech patterns, pronunciations, word choices, and more can set people apart. Even if you speak English with an American accent, there are further variations on the language, depending on what part of the country you're from. Do most Americans feel camaraderie with other Americans? In a country of immigrant descendants, I have observed camaraderie in America often stems more from shared heritage—such as ancestral roots or lived experiences—than from simply being American.

America is often spoken of as a melting pot, but more accurately, it's a salad bowl. Throughout American history, lots of people came here from lots of different parts of the world, and while it's true we're all jumbled together somewhat like a salad, traditionally ethnicities and races didn't mix together and "melt" into the proverbial pot. The change we are witnessing now is the evolution of this country from a salad bowl into a true melting pot. We are now becoming a country (among many other developed countries) that's experiencing the blending of ethnicities on a large scale. One day, it will be nearly impossible to segregate society by race or color in the ways we have historically done. So, what will that mean for feeling incognito? If everyone in the future becomes a combination of multiple ethnicities, will we all feel more comfortable or less comfortable around one another? Will we feel more or less comfortable in our own skin?

My hope is that the more we blend cultures, the more open we will become to learning about and understanding ways of communicating, ways of behaving, and ways of living that are outside what we might be accustomed to. Instead of focusing on blending in with others ("I worry about how I might be perceived as different,"), I hope we will become more focused on celebrating the unique attributes of others ("I celebrate how someone is different,"). Being around others will become less about changing who we are to accommodate what we believe to be the norm, and more about observing, understanding, and finding points of connection that may be less obvious to the eye.

I do wish I had engaged further in conversation with my seatmate on the flight. We made a little small talk, but upon reflection, that moment would have been a perfect opportunity for me to quickly educate myself on some of the customs in Thai culture, the highlights of local cuisine, and so much more. It was such a missed opportunity for connection, because the conversation started with a spotlight on what made me different in an exclusionary way rather than focusing on what made this stranger unique in an inclusive way. What hobbies might we have had in common that could have led me to an incredible, off the beaten path local experience?

When others ask about me, I should, in turn, ask about them. Every conversation is an opportunity for mutual learning. And even when people look the same, dress the same, and speak the same language, their lived experiences are rarely the same. We are all uniquely different.

## Communication Across Cultural Lines

My personal experiences with overt racism have luckily been few and far between, which I attribute to my being racially ambiguous, as someone once called me. What they meant was that no one can ever tell what race I am. It's only clear I'm not white, but even then, at a glance, some may think I could be partially Caucasian. When I lived in New York City, people would often walk up to me on the street speaking in a language other than English, expecting me to respond. More than once, with a look of awkwardness on my face, I had to say, "No hablo español" (i.e., "I don't speak Spanish"), after someone divulged an emotion-filled story in quickly spoken Spanish I couldn't understand. New York City has many Spanish speakers, so I learned a few very simple responses, but when the same scenario occurred in languages other than Spanish, it just led to moments of even greater awkwardness as I tried to communicate via body language and facial expressions that I only speak English and would not be able to assist them.

I find it funny today that my husband speaks fluent Spanish, but by his clearly non-Hispanic appearance, you would never guess it. There's a small Colombian restaurant near my church that we enjoy going to for breakfast from time to time, and whenever we're seated there, the server looks at me and immediately starts speaking in Spanish. Of course, I rely on my husband to respond, as they are often speaking too quickly for me to even try to comprehend the words. The server's reaction is always priceless when they realize my husband is fluent, but I'm not. We can't help but laugh every time.

While I admit it would benefit me to learn a language other than English, I'm thankful for the technology available today that allows me to communicate across language barriers. There's one experience I had with technology-assisted translation I will never forget. When I was in my mid-twenties, I was traveling with my parents, and our flight was delayed. There were multiple announcements made by the gate attendant, but they were made only in English. The delay became so severe the airline offered food vouchers to all passengers, but you needed to line up at the gate's desk to claim them, of course. I watched everyone in the immediate area step forward to create a long line—everyone except for one family of two adults and two children.

As more updates were announced, I watched this family continue to sit, unfazed by the activity happening around them. Something in me decided to walk over and make sure they had heard the announcements, as the changes undoubtedly would have a serious effect on their travel plans. The wife informed me in very limited English that she and her family spoke Portuguese, and it was clear she didn't understand most of what I was saying. So, I pulled out my smartphone and searched for the Google Translate app. Once I downloaded it, I typed phrases and sentences into the app and then played the Portuguese translation on the speaker; I watched as the parents' eyes went wide at hearing all the updates for the first time. The wife looked at me and said, "Thank you," before racing to the counter to speak to an airline representative.

A little while later, after cashing in our meal voucher in the food court, I saw the family scurrying to another gate. I assumed they got rebooked on another flight. The woman saw me with my family and waved frantically, saying "Thank you," many times while ushering her small children towards their gate and urging them to move faster.

It was a simple observation of the family's behavior that led me to assist them, and I often wonder what the world would be like if we all took positive action on our simple observations. I don't always act on my thoughts, but I was so glad I did that day. Just by looking at the family, I wouldn't have identified them as non-American, and I would have assumed they spoke English. Their indistinguishable appearance probably served them well in some ways while traveling, but in this particular instance, it almost did them a disservice.

It's important to note that although speaking different languages is one type of communication barrier, there are other challenges that can prevent us from communicating effectively across cultures. Often the barrier is simply not having a certain level of comfort with the person to whom you are speaking—this discomfort may prevent you from being able to express yourself freely. Comfort across cultures is one superpower of being multiracial I thoroughly enjoy. The ability to create an authentic level of comfort across racial and ethnic barriers allows me to be a "translator" of sorts, opening up new perspectives to those who might not otherwise consider alternative views. Growing up in a predominantly white area expanded my opportunities to translate between cultures, because I was able to gain the trust and respect of those outside of my race; that, in turn, created a level of vulnerability in conversation that would otherwise not have existed.

Amid the Black Lives Matter protests of 2016, and in the lead-up to the first election of Donald Trump as president of the US, I had an old classmate from high school reach out to me via Facebook Messenger. She had seen a heated exchange I'd had publicly with a mutual friend on his Facebook page, where I was asking to take the conversation offline; I wanted to have a rational conversation about what I believed was propaganda and disinformation. He ignored my request, and the flames of divisive discourse only further ignited in a very public forum. When I disengaged from the exchange, my old friend reached out. She said she realized I wasn't asking to talk to her personally, but that she was genuinely interested in understanding where I was coming from.

In the spirit of transparency, I must say I knew this woman, but she and I were never close. Her request caught me off guard, but I was happy (and excited) to connect for an honest conversation. When we managed to find time for a phone call, she opened up to me, saying she felt she was in a weird position all the time from growing up in a family who claimed not to be racist but whose actions said otherwise. She told me what it was like to try to change their perceptions. She expressed all the emotional fatigue she felt from internally battling with herself: When was it worth it to push a point, and when was there too much at stake personally to keep going? I admired her bravery and persistence towards allyship, as proven by her seeking out the opportunity to talk with me.

She said she didn't have very many Black friends, and she had no family members of color, so she was thankful for opportunities to get out of the echo chamber that everyone around her was so comfortable in. I wished more people shared in her curiosity and yearning for exposure to diverse perspectives, but I was also thankful she felt assured I would provide a safe space for open conversations about hard topics. She prefaced the call by saying up front that she wanted to talk to learn, and that she hoped her ignorance wouldn't be mistaken for indifference or a desire to ignore the lived realities of others. Her openness to learn was exactly what I had been seeking from our mutual friend on Facebook, but his pride and "sense of Confederate heritage" wouldn't allow for it. I, too, wanted to learn from his lived experience, but unfortunately, he wouldn't give me a chance.

One door closed was another door opened, and I'm thankful for the opportunity that was created for me to chat openly with someone else from our little Southern town. I consider it a privilege to be invited into hard conversations with people who are not used to speaking openly about race. I have definitely gone through phases when talking about race becomes exhausting, but these conversations are important, and I know those who came before me endured confrontation that went far beyond just words. So, while speaking up and speaking out might be exhausting, it's also progress.

## Dual Citizenship

One thing about being the child of an immigrant is that you might have the option to become a citizen of both your parents' homeland and the US. I have friends who have even been able to get dual citizenship through their grandparents' country of origin. Two of my American friends have applied for and received citizenship in Ireland by providing proof of descent, and they were able to retain their US citizenships, too. How advantageous to be granted rights as a citizen in two different countries.

Having traveled and lived abroad in various parts of the world, I now recognize there are many different ways to live. In America's capitalistic society, we put a lot of emphasis on career and gaining wealth. Money is our primary driver, and thus more time at work is the norm. I have witnessed a different way of life in other parts of the world, where rest and time spent with family are prioritized. In Spain and Italy, many businesses shut down in the afternoon for what is known as *siesta* or *riposo*. This is a time to go home, rest, and be with family. The origin of this custom is in agriculture, when workers needed to get out of the sun at the peak heat of the day and rest. I love that this tradition is still a cultural practice, even in modern economies where many people don't need a break from the sun because they work indoors. The reality is we all could use a break from work during the midday hours to refresh our minds and spend time with people we care about.

Becoming a dual citizen seems to me like taking one step towards becoming a citizen of the world. Familiarizing yourself with various cultures and ways of life affords you more freedom to choose what kind of life you want to live, simply by way of awareness. Without such awareness, a lack of knowledge will make life choices for you. So many doors open through dual citizenship.

While an American passport is one of the best, there are perks to having dual citizenship. My friends with Irish passports are now members of the European Union, meaning they can travel visa-free to any country in the EU. Plus, they will have additional consular protection while traveling, even if they're outside of the EU.

Dual citizenship can also open up business opportunities. Citizenship in a country has implications for your ability to secure paid work, own property, enter into business agreements, be exempt from certain taxes, and so much more.

Access to greater healthcare and education options can also be improved by dual citizenship, but many people never take time to explore the options that exist outside of the US. Our systems are expensive in comparison to many other places around the world. Healthcare in other countries is certainly worth researching, especially if you have the option to apply for dual citizenship. This is not to say that you won't find even more expensive or competitive systems in other countries, but there are some places in the world where both healthcare and education are considered rights and not privileges.

Unfortunately for me, Malaysia does not allow dual citizenship. To become a Malaysian citizen, you have to renounce your previous nationality. Since I don't have plans to permanently relocate to Malaysia, I thought it would be best not to pursue citizenship there any further, especially given all the rights and privileges American citizenship provides.

While I've focused on the positives so far, it should be noted that there could also be less-ideal consequences to consider for dual citizens. In some countries, there are military obligations associated with citizenship. There also might be restrictions on the type of work you are able to perform or the religion you practice. Dual taxation could be a new burden of responsibility.

There are many factors to consider, but the point I'd like to stress is that many of us have options to change our citizenship or add to the list of countries where we have citizenship. In this interconnected world where you have access to information from across the globe and from a variety of sources, the possibilities for who you can become are endless. There are so many opportunities to travel and live abroad that if you want to explore your roots, or even return to them permanently, doing so is probably more attainable than you think.

Eventually, maybe there will be an opportunity to simply be a citizen of the world. A time might come when we will be able to move around the globe as we see fit and still receive the care and protection we need, all while being given opportunities to meaningfully contribute to the places we visit, regardless of where we were born. I would like to think that not only will the opportunities be there, but also that our enthusiasm for taking advantage of those opportunities will be welcomed.

# PART III:

# LOVE, LABOR, AND LEGACY

People don't need to mirror your experience to understand you. THEY JUST NEED TO LISTEN.

Dating Qualifications:

- ☑ Nice smile
- ☑ Good reputation
- ☑ Kind person
- ☒ Same race
- ☒ Same religion

Strong relationships are built on good communication.

Employee Resource Groups: Voluntary, employee-led groups whose aim is to foster a diverse, inclusive workplace aligned with the organizations they serve.

2009: Barack Obama becomes the first mixed race U.S. President

>>> The success of AI should be measured by how intelligently and COMPASSIONATELY we use this technology to shape our world. <<<

2018: Meghan Markle becomes the first mixed race member of the British royal family.

"You two are going to have the most beautiful mulatto babies!"

"You one of them redbones."

2020: Black Lives Matter
+ Asian hate due to COVID
= Isolated in so many ways

Strong, lasting community ties creates a sense of belonging.

Today I'm thankful for:

- ♡ curly hair products
- ♡ skin tone bandaids
- ♡ skin tone undergarments
- ♡ skin tone colored pencils

# CHAPTER 7

# Dating & Relationships

## *My "Type"*

I AM SO blessed to be married to a kind, caring, smart, and capable person. My husband Alex is without a doubt the man of my dreams, and though it took thirty-five years for me to find him, he was well worth the wait.

Our lived experiences could not be more different, but we communicate well, and as a result, we are constantly learning from one another. Back when I was single and I said, "I want someone who understands me," I assumed I meant someone who had walked a path similar to mine and could directly relate to the way I see the world. Instead, it turns out people don't need to mirror your experience to understand you—they just need to listen, like my husband does. They need to listen to understand and not to respond. When someone hears you, they get to know you. After some time getting to know you, they understand who you are, how you internalize your experiences, and how best to support you on your journey.

Prior to meeting my husband, I found dating to be an exhausting and misleading series of events. As I got older, it only got harder. This perplexed me because, with more experience, aren't things supposed to get easier? Yet, instead of feeling more confident when dating, I found myself grappling with the same frustrations on repeat and wondering why my life was less like a romantic comedy and more like a comedy of errors.

In the movie *Stomp the Yard*, there's a scene where Zoe Saldaña's character says, "Southern girls don't date. We have boyfriends." This was my sentiment exactly. In my mind, dating represented curiosity, whereas a serious relationship represented comfort. But for me, by my thirties, I was done being curious, because I truly felt as though I had dated men of all sorts: Black, white, tall, short, Asian, Jewish—no one was necessarily out of the question. Looking back at the men I've dated, I would have to say there isn't a single thing that links them all together. I would even venture to assert I don't have a "type," as I believe everyone is attractive in their own unique way. Besides, it's not until you get to know someone that you really know what they look like. You would be surprised at the number of ugly people I've met who, at first, appeared to be quite attractive.

As I've mentioned, I grew up in a predominately white small town. In order to maximize my potential dating pool, I never considered limiting myself to only dating men of my own race. And if I did, what would that even mean? Would that be inclusive of anyone who was Black *or* Asian? Or would my dates need to be Black *and* Asian? If the latter, then I knew I was destined to be alone, at least through high school graduation.

Navigating questions about my own identity in the context of dating has always been complex. Adding to this, the history of interracial dating and marriage in the US reflects the significant legal and social barriers many couples (especially

Black-white couples) have faced to be together. Anti-miscege-nation laws banned interracial marriage in many states until the 1967 Supreme Court case *Loving vs. Virginia* overturned them. While acceptance has grown over time, there are still traces of historical prejudices today.

As a product of my parents' interracial marriage, inter-racial dating seemed perfectly normal to me. Apparently, not everyone felt this way, including people I was close to. In high school, I revealed to a friend that I was interested in dating our mutual friend, who was Black. Her response was, "I'd definitely date him… if I could date a Black guy." My mind exploded. I was shocked by the comment because I'd never heard her say anything like that before, but when I thought about it more, I realized she had never dated a Black guy—and frankly, neither had I. I guess it had never been a topic of discussion because it just never came up.

This was a girl I had known my whole life. She was one of the few friends whose parents had become friends with my parents—my parents weren't really the socializing type when it came to their children's friends. However, this girl had been a close friend since kindergarten, and our parents met on so many occasions that their friendship was inevitable. To this day, her parents are among the nicest people I know. They have been, and continue to be, like second parents to me. It blows my mind thinking that they wouldn't approve of their children dating peo-ple outside of their own race.

I later learned they weren't the only ones who felt this way. Another of my best friends from childhood was a tall Cauca-sian boy. Very smart. Very athletic. Very good looking. None of

117

these things mattered to me growing up, because this boy, who I'll call Ted, was one of my best friends, almost like a brother to me. I couldn't and wouldn't look at him any other way, and our friendship lasted through high school. But later, when I was in my early twenties, I talked to an old high school boyfriend of mine, and he told me about an incident that occurred right before we started dating. He knew I was good friends with Ted, and when we were all in high school together, he had approached Ted in the locker room after football practice to ask him why he had never dated me himself. Ted's response was not at all what I expected. When girls asked me the same question about him, I would say, "Because Ted's like a brother to me, and that's gross." Ted's response, however, was, "Because my dad would kill me." I knew Ted's dad and got along with the man just fine, or so I thought. It was then I learned that sometimes race outweighs relationships.

I still wonder if both of these friends' parents really thought this way, or if my friends just assumed they did. Neither of my friends ever tested those theories, and now they're both married to spouses of their same race. If their parents did in fact feel that way, I also wonder if time has changed their minds.

Beyond just parental approval, I found out in college that even my peers from outside of the American South were prone to putting up dating barriers based on cultural differences. In a place as diverse as Manhattan, however, things were no longer just about Black and white. During my sophomore year, there was a Muslim guy of Middle Eastern descent on the soccer team who sparked my interest. As a member of the dance team, many of the people in my social circle were involved in collegiate

athletics, and this young man was no exception. While our social circles overlapped, I didn't know him well. All I knew was
he had a great smile and was really kind when we ran into each
other on campus. He was also clearly well-respected by his team-
mates. When I mentioned my budding crush to a mutual friend,
she immediately discouraged me from pursuing it any further. I
was Christian, he was Muslim—the two shall never fall in love.
Those weren't her exact words, but they might as well have been.
Without questioning it, I took her advice and tucked my love
interest away for good.

I don't wonder what would have resulted from my dating
any of the aforementioned men, but I do wonder if there are still
young people who are being discouraged from dating someone
due to lingering historical prejudices or unfounded assumptions
about their chances of success. Perhaps the true challenge isn't
just in overcoming the biases of others, but in learning to reject
the narratives that tell us who we should or shouldn't love. That
way, we can define connection on our own terms.

## Learning From My Parents

They say a woman tends to marry someone who reminds
her of her father. My husband may not look like my father, but
there are definitely characteristics about him that are similar to
my dad. I find them in the way he takes care of me. For instance,
Alex is always thinking about my safety. Whether I'm climbing a
ladder to reach something or getting in the car to go somewhere,
he is quick to offer help. Also, he stays on top of any potential issues with my car so that I'm always in a safe and well-maintained

vehicle. These are small but still significant things I have seen my dad do for my mom over and over again.

The two most important men in my life appear quite different. My dad is loud, and my husband is quiet. My dad is intensely into sports, while my husband does watch sports here and there, he doesn't keep up with every game. My dad is not afraid of conflict, while my husband prefers to avoid it, opting for calm and compromise whenever possible. Yet once you get to know them, their similarities rise to the surface. They both prioritize savings and security. They both highly value self-reliance and respect. They will both have you where you need to be on time, because one thing they aren't is late for an appointment.

In building and shaping my own marriage, I often look to my parents' relationship. My parents had an unspoken arrangement that my mom would take care of chores inside the house, and my dad would take care of responsibilities outside of the house (meaning yard work and the cars). Of course, my sister and I had chores sprinkled in on both fronts to lighten the load, but you could think of my parents as the managers of their assigned domains. The system worked well for them. As a result, Alex and I have a similar arrangement.

I learned a lot from watching my parents' marriage growing up. Their personalities are very different, and they have learned to live life together accordingly. When they get into arguments, it's always particularly interesting. When my dad gets emotional, he gets louder, but when my mom gets emotional, she shuts down all communication. She needs time to walk away and process, whereas my dad processes by venting and letting it all out. This created a lot of tension in their arguments when

I was younger, but now their disagreements are resolved in a much calmer manner because they have learned to communicate better and respect how the other person wants and needs to be treated.

Navigating differences in personality traits is one thing, but navigating cultural differences is another. For example, my dad loves sarcasm and has a big sense of humor. His sarcasm isn't always something my mom will pick up on, probably because she wasn't born and raised in America. Sarcasm is more than just the words you say, it's also the tone of your delivery, your word choice, and the greater context of the conversation. Even someone fluent in English like my mom might not pick up on these additional cues, and I can't count the number of times my dad has made a sarcastic joke that went right over my mom's head. Over the years, she has learned to almost look for his sarcasm, but even still sometimes she misses it, so my dad uses a lot of that content with me and my sister instead. He can usually get a good laugh out of us.

Another way my parents navigate cultural differences is in how they approach decision-making. My mom often focuses on what's best for the collective, which I attribute to her upbringing, as this perspective is common in many Asian cultures. She rarely prioritizes her own desires, instead defaulting to the needs of the family or the group as a whole. My dad, on the other hand, sometimes interprets her approach as a reluctance to assert herself or her caring too much about others' opinions. His position comes from his own upbringing: African American culture, which is shaped by resilience and determination, often celebrates personal achievements and self-expression. For my parents, finding the middle ground is a balance between independence and a focus on collective identity. Neither approach is better or worse, just different.

Their relationship has taught me patience, perseverance, and the importance of clear communication. They have been married for forty-five years now, and I know it wasn't easy to get to this point. They have overcome a lot in terms of both learning how to live with one another and shaping how they move about in the world together. I am thankful to have such amazing role models to look to in my own marital journey.

## Growing Into Love

There was a moment, after I reached my thirties and was still on the dating scene, when I wished my parents would just fix me up in an arranged marriage. After all, my mother was the product of an arranged marriage. Her biological father passed away when she was young, so I guess there's no telling if that marriage would have worked out long term, but there are plenty of arranged marriages still happening around the globe that produce long-lasting, loving relationships. And who knows me better than my own parents, right?

My thought was that people can grow into love. If my parents could find a man they deemed suitable for my life partner, I was willing to get to know that man and hopefully grow to love him over time for all the reasons that my parents found him suitable in the first place. I'm glad my parents didn't take me up on that offer, or I would have missed out on falling in love with my husband, who is perfect for me and makes me blissfully happy.

However, I still believe arranged marriages are not necessarily a bad idea when they involve consenting adults.

There are so many things I wish I could have asked my maternal grandma, including her experience of an arranged marriage, as contrasted with her later experience of being in a marriage of her choosing. I had plenty of opportunities, and she was always happy to spend time talking with me, but if a topic I brought up for discussion made her even slightly uncomfortable, she would simply change the subject. (Perhaps this was a generational issue, because my paternal grandma always did the same thing.) Had I had the chance, I would have asked my mom's mom more about her views on love, and how they changed over time. Who were the greatest influences in her life when it came to love and marriage?

When I look at old photos of my parents' wedding, it's apparent that the wedding was small but not an elopement. They were married at the home of my dad's childhood pastor, and they had a small reception hosted by my grandparents after the ceremony. Dad's family was present, but Mom's family was not. This could have been due to distance, as the wedding took place in Virginia and my mom's family all live in California, but I know that was not exclusively the case. Maybe distance was the reason her siblings didn't attend, but my mom's mom didn't approve of the marriage, and thus she was not invited.

By that time, my mom's mom had long been remarried to the man I have always known as my grandfather. This was a marriage she chose, and I imagine that, after having been forced into her first marriage at a young age, it was quite a different experience getting to choose a life partner. Not only did she get to choose, but she chose a man who was Japanese American, who then brought her and her family to the US, which provided an opportunity for a better life. So, my maternal grandma was open to marrying outside of her own ethnicity and nationality, but marrying outside of her race was apparently very different in her mind. It's hard to imagine someone I loved so much, and who loved me, not approving of the union that made my life on this Earth possible.

Because Mom's side of the family lived so far away, I never really noticed if there was a strain on my dad's relationship with his in-laws, and my father says they got along well. We only saw my mom's people every few years, and the visits always seemed cordial—in fact, I'm told that, when they first met, my dad and my grandfather hit it off immediately. But my mother's side of the family is not very outwardly affectionate, which I think is just part of Asian culture. I would describe them as more stoic than emotive, so if there were any points of tension between them and my parents, it would have been hard for a child like me to detect a coldness between adults in the room. Partly because our visits were so amicable, I like to believe my grandma's love for my mom made way for a tolerance of her marriage to my dad, which then gave way to an appreciation of their union, especially once it produced grandchildren. I like to think she grew into love.

My dad's parents took the opposite approach and welcomed my mom with open arms right from the start. My paternal grandparents might not have been the most outwardly affectionate people you ever met, but they embodied Southern hospitality itself. Their house was warm and inviting, and I know my mom felt that welcoming spirit from the moment she first visited. Because of my dad's close relationship with his parents and the proximity of their homes, his parents spent time with my mom while they were dating, and my grandparents had the chance to truly get to know her. They never made any mention of her ethnicity—it simply didn't matter to them. Love was love, and it was clear their son had found his match.

In an ideal world, love would be simple and unmarred by racial tension. My hope is that as more biracial and multiracial children populate the Earth, more and more people will find opportunities to grow into love with those they might not have been open to getting to know. It's also my hope that more and more people take my dad's parent's approach, embracing love at face value, regardless of racial and ethnic lines.

## "The One"

When I was dating in my twenties, I remember thinking I might never find someone who would accept me for who I am. Someone who would feel comfortable around both sides of my family. Someone who would appreciate my various quirks that stem from a variety of cultural influences and make me who I am.

I grew up wearing Timberland boots on one day, and cowboy boots on another. The radio preset stations included channels for pop, hip-hop, and country. And I can't forget the button that filled the car with smooth jazz and R&B, an ode to memories in the car with my dad.

My culinary habits worried me most when it came to finding "the one," because who, besides my own sister, could possibly eat like I eat? Who would like and feel comfortable with some of the snacks and meals I grew up on that were often far from what you'd typically find at a restaurant? Even before a willingness to eat with me, "the one" would also have to bear some of the more pungent scents (fish sauce, anyone?) my foods produced. Both my grandmas were the type to feed you until you couldn't eat any more, but their cuisines were very different. And it wasn't just *their* kitchens I worried about, but also my own. I was known to flip an egg in a pan, place it over a plate of white rice, add a dash of soy sauce, and call that breakfast. While Americans don't typically eat rice for breakfast, my mom ate rice with every meal, so my sister and I learned to do the same.

I knew my husband was the one for me when the topic of dace came up, because he was familiar with dace and was excited to eat it with me. For those who aren't acquainted with this dish, dace is a type of freshwater carp that's fried and canned with salted black beans in oil. It's not found in your everyday grocery store, but it's a staple in Asian food markets. The fish have a chewy, almost jerky-like texture, and even the bones are edible (well, the small ones, anyway). The fermented black beans are little pockets bursting with flavor, extremely salty and extremely satisfying. My mom used to keep cans of dace in the pantry when we were kids, and she would prepare it for herself if she wasn't in the mood for whatever American dish she'd fixed for the rest of us to enjoy for dinner. It was a treat when I would get to have some as well, as dace was Mom's special pantry item. Little did I know dace is actually a cheap meal, but to my eye as a child, it was a delicacy only to be enjoyed on rare occasions with Mom.

The fact that Alex knew what dace was and wasn't repulsed by it was a big green light for me. I thought acceptance of my pulling together various snacks into a meal and calling it dinner would be the stretch goal for finding a partner who understood me. A partner who liked dace was a level I thought unattainable for sure.

It saddens me that neither of my grandmas lived long enough to meet my husband. They would have loved him, and he would have loved them. I try to keep them alive through sharing stories with him when something reminds me of one grandma or the other. We keep our loved ones alive in our hearts by reveling in their memories.

## Wedding Traditions

Engagement is both an exciting and an overwhelming time in life. There is so much to look forward to, and there are also *so* many decisions to make. How many people will you invite? Who will and will not make the list? Where will you get married? Who will you ask to be in your bridal party? What will the color scheme of your wedding be? The list goes on and on, and it can change dramatically with cultural influences.

As someone who got married in her mid-thirties, I had the pleasure of attending and taking part in numerous weddings before it was my turn to walk down the aisle. At each wedding, I made mental notes of the things I loved and the things I thought weren't worth the cost (which were most things, honestly). I also talked to my mom a lot about my observations and what she could expect to see or not see on my special day.

I will admit my wedding was not at all what I envisioned throughout the many years that I had served as a bridesmaid for my friends. Because we grew up close to my dad's side of the family and went to church every Sunday, I always imagined having a large church wedding. American Southern tradition tells you the bride's parents are responsible for paying for the wedding, while the groom's parents are responsible for the rehearsal dinner. My dad made it very clear to both me and my sister when we were young that he would be paying for zero weddings, but that he would be there to help with more reasonable large investments, like the down payment on a house. It's not that he doesn't value marriage, it's that he believes the party to celebrate the union shouldn't be lavish and cost thousands upon thousands of dollars. So, when I was old enough to realize how much a large church wedding would cost (because you just *have* to have a big reception afterward with an open bar), my vision for my own wedding began to shift.

As a result of the COVID-19 pandemic, small weddings and elopements became more acceptable. My husband proposed towards the end of the pandemic, so we took this as an opportunity to keep the guest list short. Neither of our families is much for tradition, so we decided to have a destination wedding. Our wedding quickly turned into a weeklong family-and-friends-vacation to Costa Rica—all for the same price we would have paid for the more traditional wedding I had dreamed of in my younger years. Having a destination wedding with such a small guest list was one of the best decisions we have ever made. I highly recommend it.

While we went an extremely untraditional route for the wedding overall, there were traditions I considered when we were planning the ceremony. I had always thought about "jumping the broom," mostly because I'd seen it in movies and thought it was a wonderful idea. I liked the sentiment of honoring my African and African American ancestors through this tradition that enslaved people brought with them from West Africa. (Many enslaved people were not allowed to legally wed, so jumping the broom became a symbol of marital union.) Similarly, while working at the resort in Malaysia, I had the pleasure of being on staff at a wedding which brought together an Australian groom and an Indian bride. At Indian weddings, families of the bride and groom exchange gifts as a sign of respect and appreciation. While I'm not of Indian heritage, I absolutely adore the idea of not just welcoming a new son-in-law or daughter-in-law to the family, but also welcoming the family members they bring with them. While we didn't end up jumping the broom or exchanging gifts between families at our wedding, these are beautiful, time-honored traditions I am so thankful to know about and have witnessed.

As a child of mixed heritage, I'm sure there are many more wedding-related traditions from those who have come before me that I am still unaware of. I would urge young people reading this to ask questions of their family members to reveal traditions from their weddings and from their cultures that they might want to incorporate into their special day when it comes. Or, there may even be an opportunity to blend traditions or start new ones.

There is so much we can learn through the traditional behaviors that are passed down from generation to generation. They can reveal values and tell stories, and by continuing those traditions, we keep those memories alive. By sharing them with people from other walks of life, we humanize unfamiliar cultures and build bridges. Food is one of the most popular things humans gravitate toward for connection across racial and ethnic lines, but love is also something everyone can understand and appreciate. Wedding traditions are just some of the various creative ways in which we choose to express that love.

# CHAPTER 8

# Professional Identity & Workplace Dynamics

## *Miss Priss Tea*

WHEN I WAS in graduate school, one of my professors had us write our own eulogies. The point of the assignment was to draw from it the things we wanted to be remembered for. It was a life lesson in making sure we give our time and energy not just to our profession, but to what really matters in life. For each person, "what really matters" can mean something different, but for me, this means family. I wrote my eulogy from the perspective of my best friend, who was waxing poetic about my return to Virginia after having lived all over the world, then having fulfilled my dream of opening a tearoom. (I love afternoon tea.) In my eulogy, I talked about involving my mother and daughter in the tearoom business. (Although I don't have any children, in my pretend future I was a mom.) To me, owning a business was about creating something lasting—something that could benefit my family for generations to come.

My love for afternoon tea came about because of my travels. I'd had afternoon tea experiences while living in New York City, but also while studying abroad as an undergrad in the Czech Republic and traveling all across Europe that semester. My favorite afternoon tea experience came just after I finished my graduate semester abroad in Japan. I had traveled to Myanmar with friends before returning home, and we went to high tea at the Strand Hotel in Yangon. Their tea service was a blend of traditional English afternoon tea with traditional Myanmar delicacies, so while we enjoyed finger sandwiches with the crusts cut off and dainty pastries, we also enjoyed steamers full of dim sum. This was my heaven.

Inspired by the eulogy assignment, I returned home to Virginia shortly after finishing my MBA. While I didn't have the money to open a brick-and-mortar tearoom, I did have the resources and energy to test my business idea by launching a mobile tea party catering business. During my travels, I had started building a small mismatch collection of English bone china from thrift stores, and I continued collecting once I got home. When I had enough place settings to host tea for twenty people, I began inviting family and friends to partake in the experience and provide feedback. Without the overhead of an office or a physical tearoom, the startup costs were low. And, as was written in my made-up eulogy, my mom was more than happy to act as my right-hand lady both in the kitchen and when providing table service to my event attendees. It was a small two-person operation to start, but that was all we needed. Tea is a time-honored tradition in many places outside of the US, and I wanted to bring tea culture back home with me.

For three years, I ran a tea party events company, Miss Priss Tea, which offered a traditional English-style afternoon tea experience at a venue of the client's choosing. We catered book clubs, birthday parties, bridal showers, and more, but the business never took off enough to provide me with full-time employment. One of the most fun events we ever hosted was a global tea tasting at a coworking space for women. The tasting was three courses, and each course was a small introduction to a tea experience from a different part of the world, complete with a traditional accompaniment of small bites. We started with Japanese tea, then moved to Turkish tea, and we finished with an English tea service. It was a sold-out event and a great learning experience for all.

I still dream of creating a more sustainable business plan that would allow me to open a teahouse offering global tea experiences at affordable price points. My dream teahouse would have different rooms you could move through to take part in various teatime traditions. For instance, you might experience a Chinese *Gongfu* tea ceremony in one room, which focuses on brewing *oolong* or *pu-erh* tea using small teapots, multiple short infusions, and precise control of water temperature. As you walk past the next room over, you might smell the fresh mint leaves from a Moroccan tea ceremony as guests sip slowly from ornate glasses. Then, down the hall, others might partake in a Russian *zavarka* tea tradition, where there would be a variety of jams to add to their tea, along with *pryaniki* (spice cookies) to enjoy. Traditions around tea are diverse and wonderful, and I want to continue sharing these cultural traditions with any and all who are interested.

Despite my love of afternoon tea, growing up, I really only knew three types of tea. The first and most familiar was Southern sweet tea. My paternal grandma always had a pitcher (or two) in the fridge, and it was my drink of choice. Knowing what I know now about tea and its many varieties, the tea that I knew as a child was more like sugar water than actual tea. There was certainly black tea in it, but there was only a hint of tea flavor in the beverage—it was mostly sugar. I still laugh when I go out with my parents today, because no matter where we're dining, at any place around the world, my dad will always ask if they have Southern sweet tea. Despite it being a very American (and more specifically, very Southern) beverage, he always keeps hope alive that Southern sweet tea will have caught on far outside the confines of the American South.

The two other teas I would have on occasion while growing up were chrysanthemum tea and jasmine tea. These were the types of tea served at a typical sit-down Chinese restaurant. I always preferred the chrysanthemum tea because it's naturally sweeter, and because I liked the idea of drinking tea made from flowers. Jasmine tea is also made from flowers, but I didn't know that since the tiny jasmine buds were less obvious when I peered into the teapot—the chrysanthemum tea was made with bigger, bright yellow flowers.

Learning from her mother-in-law, my mom also regularly kept a pitcher of Southern sweet tea in the fridge (and still does to this day). That was the only tea we really ever had in the house. I didn't get into brewing hot tea until my college years, when I started spending a lot of time at coffee shops and realized drinking coffee made me nauseous. (This is still the case today, although I have never looked into the cause). So, part of my inspiration for getting into afternoon tea and seeking out other teatime experiences was simply my search for opportunities to meet with friends over a beverage that wasn't coffee or alcohol.

Returning home from graduate school and starting Miss Priss Tea gave me an opportunity to educate others, using tea as a way of bridging cultures. Although my business centered on the tradition of English afternoon tea rather than other tea customs, I quickly realized many people from my hometown were unfamiliar with this iconic tea experience. In an increasingly casual and digital world, my customers often expressed their gratitude for an opportunity to dress up a little and spend quality time in face-to-face conversations with others without feeling rushed to give up their seats to the next round of waiting customers. This was about more than teaching the formal traditions of English tea (such as gently stirring in the sugar with a half-circle motion as opposed to swirling your spoon all the way around); it was about introducing a mindset and way of life that contrasts with the fast-paced, productivity-obsessed culture we've grown so accustomed to.

I was so excited to be able to host afternoon tea on May 19, 2018, the day when Prince Harry married Meghan Markle, making her the first modern mixed-race member of the British royal family. Since the livestream of the wedding took place at 5:00 a.m. local time, I recorded it to play on a loop at my tea event later in the day. But rest assured, I was awake, dressed, and event-prepping while watching the wedding in real time. It was like watching a real-life fairytale.

Tea inspires me in more ways than one. I have a painting in my living room of two young Black girls having afternoon tea with their stuffed animals. The painting was given to me by my former boss because she knew I loved teatime. (I ran Miss Priss Tea while working full time during the week for the nonprofit she was the executive director of.) The painting was passed down to her, and after her daughter expressed no interest in it, my boss offered it to me, which I thought was very kind. It hangs above my tea cart, where I keep many varieties of tea and a selection of my most-used tea-ware. I boil hot water every morning in my electric kettle here.

The painting of the two girls was the inspiration for a project I started to put together but was never able to bring to fruition. The painting is one of the few I have seen depicting Black people doing what I consider to be more affluent activities. Inspired by this, I dreamed of creating a traveling art exhibit that featured pieces showing Black men, women, and children living lives of wealth. An example might be a painting of Black couples relaxing on a yacht. While there are certainly Black people living luxurious lives, I wanted that lifestyle represented in art and showcased where young Black people could see it. Representation is everything.

This was an effort I started just before the COVID-19 pandemic, which is where the idea lost steam. I had reached out to a handful of local artists to gauge interest in the project, and I'd had a few takers. What I needed was a space for the initial exhibition, a strong title for the series, and a grand marketing plan. Having grown up watching *The Cosby Show*, a sitcom following the life of the Huxtable family, I wanted the Huxtables' very comfortable lifestyle (or higher) to be represented in the exhibit, as the characters on the show were a vision of Black excellence on television. My idea was Black excellence on canvas, so I had tentatively named the exhibition *How to Huxtable*. Unfortunately, some of the feedback I received said attaching the exhibit to anything related to Bill Cosby—who is today more closely associated with his real-life sexual assaults and misconduct than with his television persona as a wholesome role model—was bad for business. While I agree, I can't help but mourn the fact that one of the few shining examples from my childhood of Black success both domestically and professionally (in the show, the husband was a doctor and the wife a lawyer) has been tainted forever by the reprehensible behavior of a single actor—unfortunately the namesake of the show.

## *The Sting of Nostalgia*

It's strange growing up in a place with such a rich, often painful, history. There's a constant tension between appreciating the beauty of Virginia's heritage and grappling with the deep scars left by its fraught racial past. During the Civil War, Richmond proudly served as the capital of the Confederacy—and the state will never let you forget it. I grew up with classmates who participated in Civil War reenactments alongside multiple generations of their family. Schools, streets, neighborhoods, parks, and monuments honoring Confederate leaders were everywhere. While many of these symbols have been removed or renamed in recent years, their legacy remains embedded in the state's architecture, museums, and cultural identity. Maybe that's why I didn't particularly like history class as a kid.

Someone once told me their least favorite assignment in school was being asked to dress up as their favorite US president. The person telling the story was Black, and I can understand why she might have found the assignment particularly frustrating as a child. At that point in time, there hadn't been a single American president who looked even remotely like her, and it would have taken either a lot of effort or a lot of imagination for her to pull off a costume that would prompt her classmates to guess who she might be.

While those kinds of assignments are common enough, it never interested me to think about what my life would be like in a different era of history. Today—right now, in 2025—is the best it has ever been for someone like me: Black, Asian, female, and full of hopes and dreams. I live in a time when those hopes and dreams are actually achievable, unlike in the past, when any success I achieved would likely have been met with significant resistance and even hardship.

Similarly, I can't tell you how many times I've been asked, as an icebreaker or part of a dinner party conversation, "If you could live in any era, which would you choose?" Because I'm me, I always reply, "this one," and I try to leave it at that. It's an innocent question every time it's posed, and I never make a scene about it, but to go back in time would diminish my quality of life and perceived self-worth. Because I don't want to ruffle any feathers, I often don't mention what I think or how I feel about the weight of such a question. I either give it a short answer or avoid the inquiry altogether, changing the subject. I like being me—in the here and now—and I recognize that, in any other era, my existence wouldn't have been possible. (Okay, maybe it would've been *possible*, but there was a very slim chance of it.) The various parts that make me who I am include the ethnicities and cultures that are inherent to my being.

Even if I don't want to live in another era, I understand history is important. I once met a very accomplished Black female leader in Richmond, who went on to become the Executive Director of the Jamestown-Yorktown Foundation, an organization which preserves Virginia's colonial history through their living history museum. In her younger years, she was one of the first Black reenactors in historic Colonial Williamsburg, which is another of Virginia's living history museums. She went on to establish herself as a highly regarded leader in the world of museum administration, and she even led the American Civil War Museum in Richmond for a time. I became a museum member during her tenure because I saw the way she approached storytelling within the museum. It was inclusive in a way I had never seen before. She incorporated diverse perspectives, including those of African Americans, both enslaved and free, and highlighted their contributions during the Civil War. She also reinterpreted Confederate symbols, providing context and fostering dialogue about their significance, thereby creating a more inclusive and reflective narrative.

This woman was a revolutionary in her own right and still is. I'm too much of an empath to be able to do the work of preserving this country's complicated history—facing the dark truths about our country would be too much for me to bear on a day-in, day-out level. However, I realize the value of that work and the importance of having diverse perspectives and voices at the table as we impart lessons to future generations that teach how we have arrived at the culture we live in today. The work is heavy and serious, and in many cases very troubling; for me, just watching fictional movies steeped in the truths of our dark past (I'll use *Django Unchained* as an example.) makes my stomach turn and my eyes tear up.

I've never wanted to live in another era, but while running Miss Priss Tea, I would often think about how different my life would be if I had been born in an earlier time, as many of the afternoon teas I hosted took place on plantations and in colonial homes around central Virginia. I remember once going to a historic home in a wealthy neighborhood to host a private tea, and my mom joined me that day. I always loved it when she would help with my events, because it was extra time we would get to spend together, just like I had written about in my eulogy assignment. At this particular site, the house was so large there was a separate entrance for the house staff, to which we were directed. My mom whispered to me as we walked toward the side of the house with heavy bins of vintage china in tow, "I feel like the hired help going through this entrance." And I had to tell her, "We *are* the hired help."

We'd been directed to the side entrance because it was the shortest way to the kitchen, which I was grateful for as I carried thirty or so pounds of fragile tea-ware from my car into the house. But at the same time, I knew the significance of that door—the servants' entrance, the door the enslaved on the estate were relegated to. The sound of that statement coming from my mom's lips stuck with me over time because I had *chosen* to put us in such a position. It may be silly, but I believe that's part of the reason I didn't find it too hard to close up shop when the time came to move on from the business. There were several factors that went into my decision to close Miss Priss Tea, but my mom's statement and that moment were seared into the back of my mind and weighed on me heavily. I don't even think my mom meant much by saying it, but it's funny how the mind makes connections to things that evoke emotions. Until you actively recognize such a thing, you may not even realize the feelings are there or how they affect the way you think and move through the world.

## I Never Thought of You as Black

When the racial protests erupted in the summer of 2020 following the murders of George Floyd and Breonna Taylor—African Americans who were both killed by police in separate incidents—during the height of the COVID-19 pandemic, I was in a weird place mentally and emotionally. I'm an extrovert by nature, so being isolated in my house for months during lockdown was taking a real toll on me. I watched a lot of news during this period; in the midst of the global health crisis, hate crimes spiked against Asian Americans as the then-president of the US—arguably the most powerful political figure in the world—chose to place the blame for this nascent disease, and the massive disruption it caused in every facet of our lives, on the Chinese. As far as the president was concerned, anyone from China was to blame, and for many Americans, apparently that meant any Asian person was to blame.

This narrative felt so familiar. The narrative I'm referring to is one in which culturally ignorant people (mainstream America being particularly guilty of this) assume all Asian people and Asian cultures are alike, when the reality is each Asian country has its own unique culture and customs. Sometimes I wonder if that perception is in part created by Americans' affinity for Asian-fusion restaurants, of which there are a great many. You can get pad see ew (Thai cuisine) in the same restaurant that serves dim sum (Chinese cuisine) and sushi (Japanese cuisine). It's a difficult task in America to find an Asian restaurant that only serves one type of Asian cuisine. Even when a particular restaurant claims to specialize in one type of food, you will often find items on the menu from other Asian cultures. This obviously doesn't help patrons distinguish between countries and cultures at all.

While I have not eaten at nearly as many African restaurants, I have noticed those restaurants are usually thought of as Ethiopian or Moroccan or Somali, not simply labeled African. Yet despite our ability to separate African countries by cuisine, many people continue to perpetuate the myth that Africa, which is over three times the size of the US, is a country instead of a continent. According to the United Nations, fifty-four different countries make up the continent of Africa today, yet somehow when many Americans refer to anything from that continent, it is associated with all of Africa in general. Imagine if someone's only view of America was Topeka, Kansas. Now imagine being in a room with people from New York, California, and Texas and insisting they all look the same and sound the same. (These are not even different countries… these are merely different states of the same country.) This is simply to illustrate how ridiculous it is not to recognize and appreciate the many beautiful, unique cultures and peoples that come from the various countries both within Africa and Asia.

The summer of 2020 was terrifying and overwhelming to me. It seemed like Asian hate was everywhere, and being Asian American, I never knew if I would be the victim of a hate crime. Being Black, when the Black Lives Matter protests started growing in numbers and intensity, it became obvious to me that no matter which part of me someone was to see, I would still be seen as someone to hate. I couldn't win by claiming one race or the other, and even in modern-day society, my races inherently made me more vulnerable to violence. This not only frightened me, but it also frustrated me because so many people who were close to me would never be able to relate. It was isolating.

That summer, a small group of my female friends, all of whom were living in and around Richmond, decided to enjoy a little outdoor get-together. It was too risky to gather indoors, but the weather was lovely, and the Centers for Disease Control regulations allowed us to convene outside provided we socially distanced. After being on lockdown for over three months, I jumped at the opportunity for human interaction.

I'm the lone Black girl in this circle of friends, and the conversation eventually turned to the protests on Richmond's Monument Avenue. I could feel some of the women watching me specifically to see how I was reacting to the commentary on recent events. While everyone in that circle probably supported the Black Lives Matter movement, many of their parents didn't feel the same way, and some had even vocally expressed those opinions on social media. Many of these women had been part of my life since early elementary school, and their parents had been like parents to me growing up, so it was all a bit alarming to watch unfold, even if I were only watching it virtually. Now we were all face-to-face, talking through the issues as friends should, but I definitely was *not* prepared for the conversation that ensued.

What I will always remember most from that conversation is that my friends—people who I had known my entire life—collectively told me they had never "seen me as Black." My mom was always very involved with activities and events when I was in grade school, but my friends rarely saw my dad at school. Even so, they all knew he was Black. So maybe they had always thought of me as Asian? Or maybe they truly weren't thinking about race when it came to me because they just didn't find it relevant.

The idea of not viewing my race as relevant was affirmed later that afternoon when my friends told me they "had never really given it any thought." Most of the Black kids we grew up with hung out together, while I did my own thing socially speaking. I was friendly with the Black kids, but I was also friendly with everyone, and I never really showed allegiance to one group of kids over another, so maybe that's why they didn't think of me as Black. This conversation filled me with a sense of contradiction: On the one hand, it felt good to be seen as more than just the color of my skin, but at the same time, it made me feel like I wasn't fully being seen.

This discussion was the first time many of my friends had considered that although the truths about racial inequality in America revealed by the ongoing protests were news to them, they were *not* news to me. Even if racial profiling hadn't affected me directly in particularly negative ways, it affected my family and others close to me in ways no one in this group of friends would ever be able to relate to.

Honestly, I can't really blame my friends for their way of thinking—the reality is I never truly thought of myself as Black when I was young. It wasn't until my adult years that I began to see myself as both fully Asian and fully Black. I recently watched a documentary called, *1000% Me: Growing Up Mixed*, and I was so encouraged listening to the young people who were interviewed talk about how they viewed themselves. Most of these young people feel they are fully *all* the ethnicities that make up their being. I love that, and although it took me much longer than it took them to feel this way, I'm glad kids can now grow up in a world that allows them to embrace that truth.

In part because I have now fully embraced my Black heritage, for the last couple of years I have attended AfroTech, an annual conference for Black technology professionals. (I currently work full time as a technical program manager of AI-driven solutions for a global data integration and automation company.) Over 20,000 people from all over the world attend AfroTech, and it's so inspiring and energizing to be among a sea of historically marginalized people who are thriving in a growing industry that continues to both disrupt and enhance the ways in which we work, live, and play. At AfroTech, I've seen C-suite executives rotating on and off every stage, alongside certified experts and thought leaders in their respective functions who showcase what it means to embody and encourage Black excellence. A younger me would have felt out of place at a gathering of this magnitude intended solely for Black attendees, but now, whenever I'm at AfroTech and look around at the sea of faces, I see a beautiful representation of what it means to be Black. Black does not mean African American or dark-skinned or being from urban areas ... Black is a single descriptor among many that can describe an individual. Today, I feel right at home at AfroTech, and I recognize I add to the beauty of diversity within Blackness.

I've learned there is no single "Black experience." Black reflects a tapestry of experiences and ways of being. Feeling as if I am not "Black enough" has no grounds in reality. There is a higher level of melanin in my skin and African representation in my ancestry, and thus I am Black. It's not all of who I am, but it's a part of my story. And it's enough to make me feel bonded with the people at Black-centered events like AfroTech.

## Diversity in the Workplace

In my early career, I worked freelance and part-time for a variety of smaller startups, and my steady part-time job was at a live music production company. Even though I was technically working for a large corporation at the production company, I felt like I was working for a small operation, as my work environment was always in a concert venue, as opposed to a large corporate office. At every place of employment, I collaborated with a small staff of twenty or fewer individuals. In my steady part-time role, I worked alongside a diverse crew, but my freelance gigs presented a different dynamic. Interestingly, these freelance jobs often involved either a predominantly white staff or a predominantly Black staff. While I never felt out of place because of my racial identity, I did notice differences in other aspects. Notable factors were my age, as I was often significantly younger than other staff members, and my middle-class socioeconomic background, which contrasted with the wealth of my employers. These experiences marked my introduction to the working world.

It wasn't until thirteen years later that I accepted my first corporate role at a large tech company, and what an eye-opening experience that was. I was thrust into a world where there were enough people to have dedicated teams for specific functions, where my work could be taken over by someone else when I went on vacation, and where I had benefits—not just health insurance but perks like fitness reimbursement, too. Also, there were employee resource groups (ERGs) for individuals to find co-workers with shared interests and lived experiences. This was all new to me.

The ERGs were mainly geared toward bringing together and supporting minority populations in the workplace. There was one for Black employees, one for Latinx employees, one for employees in the LGBTQIA+ community, one for those living with disabilities, and the list went on. The groups were not restricted to folks who had a specific identity, as they also welcomed members who considered themselves allies. As an extrovert excited to dig into this new community of colleagues, I joined each and every group, hoping to meet a more diverse cross-section of co-workers and hopefully learn from a variety of perspectives and experiences.

It was interesting to see the number of participants in each group, the diversity represented therein, and the behaviors exhibited by members. Groups like these are intended to be safe spaces for open dialogue, but this is tricky in the workplace. For example, perhaps you join a particular group because you want to find validation and understanding since your experience at the company is not what you expected, and because you suspect the sub-par experience stems from being othered in some way. However, for obvious reasons, your reservations and feelings of otherness are probably not something you want to express in a work-based environment.

In some workplaces, I have seen two separate forums created for some of these groups. One forum is for those who personally identify with the group, and the other is for those who personally identify as well as allies. One space feels safer than the other, but the reality is all such groups are monitored by human resources and/or leadership from the organization, so anything discussed in such a group is never truly private.

Many companies use ERGs as a recruiting tool to show they are actively creating a more inclusive work environment, but I personally believe the existence of these groups doesn't necessarily mean a culture of inclusion exists. I still look for things like: How many people actively participate in these groups? What are the missions of the various groups, and how do they work to achieve them? For me, ERGs are a good start, but they're not enough to prove a company values diversity. I believe a better measure of how greatly an organization values diversity is found in a snapshot of the executive leadership and the board of directors—is there diversity among the top decision makers?

I am constantly seeking out diversity in the workplace. Any time there's an event in the works that involves a panel discussion, if I'm a part of the planning team, I help build the panel with intentional diversity—diversity of race, gender, department, and tenure with the company. The conversations are always significantly richer with a diverse panel, and I think building in diversity is well worth the extra recruitment effort. However, what I've come to notice is that many people don't think this way. When a panel is needed, some people simply put one together based on who comes to mind first, and that often equates to a very homogenous group. I find that when I raise my concern regarding diversity, I'm often met with both surprise and a joyous openness. Generally, people welcome the awareness and the opportunity; however, they often need help to find the right representation for the purpose at hand. I'm always happy to provide that service.

## Leveraging Personal Experience in a Professional Role

For nearly five years, I worked for a nonprofit organization called Leadership Metro Richmond (LMR). Founded in 1980 to address racial and gender divides in community leadership, LMR strengthens the Richmond region by connecting and empowering diverse leaders. Richmond is a city where the legacies of segregation and racial inequity remain deeply felt, yet it is also a place of progress and transformation. This duality is similar to my own experience of traversing different cultural worlds. As the Director of Communications and Programs for LMR, I was able to channel that perspective into my work, using it to benefit the broader community. My role was about more than programs and messaging—it was about creating spaces where leaders could connect, understand one another, and work toward building a more inclusive city.

As I've said, one of the greatest gifts of being multiracial is the ability to connect with people from different backgrounds. At LMR, I saw how this skill translated into building meaningful relationships across Richmond's diverse community. Whether I was facilitating conversations about systemic inequities or coordinating programs to address regional challenges, my ability to view the world through multiple lenses helped me steer my way through complex dynamics with empathy and authenticity. My goal was never to create an echo chamber, but to foster a space of vulnerability—a space where people felt safe expressing their true feelings, examining where the beliefs behind those feelings came from, and understanding why their perspective might differ from someone else's. Growing up reconciling differing cultural expectations prepared me to help others to do the same in both professional and community settings. My time at LMR also taught me leadership isn't about imposing solutions, but about listening and uniting people around shared values.

Navigating a professional role focused on cultural change in a city deeply rooted in history and tradition required being attuned to both progress and resistance. At LMR, I assisted in implementing programs designed to help leaders uncover their own biases and understand the structural inequities that shape our region. My personal experiences with challenges like these fueled my determination to advocate for initiatives which foster genuine equity and inclusion. It also better positioned me to address the region's evolving demographics by expanding the conversation beyond the traditional Black/white racial framework. As our community continues to grow, the voices of Asian and Hispanic populations must be included, ensuring that the discussions about equity reflect the full diversity of Richmond's changing landscape.

As Director of Communications and Programs, I also leaned heavily on the power of storytelling to build bridges. Growing up multiracial taught me that words and narratives matter—they can either perpetuate division or create understanding. I worked to craft messages that reflected the diversity of Richmond while honoring both its history and its potential. My experience at LMR reinforced a truth I've always known: Fostering inclusion requires more than policies or programs. It takes heart, a willingness to engage deeply, and the courage to hold space for conversations that challenge and inspire.

## Artificial Intelligence

The age of artificial intelligence is upon us, and it's creeping into every aspect of our lives. It's unavoidable, so the best thing to do is cautiously embrace it. Over the course of the last year, I have tested the capabilities of various AI models by seeing if they could produce professional headshots. In my first attempt, I paid a minimal fee to upload a few photos of myself to a particular AI tool, and in a matter of minutes, I was presented with multiple headshots to choose from. The AI managed to generate images of me wearing assorted outfits and with my hair in various styles; unfortunately, however, in many of the images something was off.

The curl type of my hair was obviously something the AI had not yet figured out, as my hair in the generated images was very curly at the ends but stick straight or wavy at the top—the transition was harsh, and it made the pictures unrealistic. There was also some obvious confusion about my ethnicity. In a number of the images, the AI had clearly mistaken my race for Indian. So, while some of the images depicted me in the corporate attire I was expecting, other photos had me in more traditional Indian attire with a sari. While I can appreciate the output's including global representations of professional headshots, this also reminded me that the instructions given in the prompt when using generative AI are important. For this particular situation, the instructions were coded into the application by the developers and not open for edits or clarification by the end user. As a user, without the ability to change the instructions or give feedback to the model, the outcomes the AI produced unfortunately did not fit my needs.

In more recent months, I've attended conferences where vendors have used AI-generated headshots as a creative way to attract attendees to their booths. The process is simple: a single photo is taken at a booth, then it's run through a generative AI model to produce a new headshot. Again, these solutions did not offer the end user the ability to edit the prompt to the AI model. As a result, I noticed these AI-driven services would often over-accentuate certain features, regardless of race or ethnicity. For instance, someone's forehead might appear disproportionately prominent, or their eyes might seem slightly bigger, giving them a more youthful but almost cartoonish appearance. At one conference, I wore my hair half up and half down, and the resulting AI-generated image gave me a bouffant hairdo that looked less like me and more like Snooki from the reality TV show *Jersey Shore*. So, while the technology is undoubtedly fun, it still falls short of creating realistic images that truly capture the nuances of a person's personality in the way a skilled photographer can. Without detailed instructions to the generative AI model that are specific to each end user and/or the intended use of the photo, it's also hard to gauge exactly what the technology is capable of in its current state. And even with great design and instructions, it's important to acknowledge that the technology is often only as effective as the person using it, just as a race-car driver's chances of winning a competition depends on their skill.

AI is reshaping not just how we interact with technology, but also how we approach problem-solving and envision the future. Just as my own diverse heritage fuels my ability to innovate, AI thrives on merging a variety of disciplines: computer science, ethics, psychology, design, and more. But AI is more than just an impressive technological advancement—it's an opportunity to build systems that truly serve a diverse and globalized world. That means creating tools which are as inclusive as they are powerful.

The racial biases often embedded in AI models are well-documented, and many individuals and organizations are working to train AI systems to be more inclusive. While current AI models are gradually improving at recognizing different ethnicities, the next frontier will be training them to detect the subtleties of blended ethnic identities like mine. This advancement could revolutionize data collection and analysis, especially as our world becomes increasingly multiracial with each generation. In fact, I believe AI has the potential to surpass human perception in understanding the intricacies of ethnic and cultural diversity.

The potential of AI extends beyond revolutionizing industries. If developed with care and intention, it can become a powerful tool for fostering understanding and equity. Technology has the ability to bridge communities, empower individuals, and help us see each other more clearly. Ultimately, the success of AI won't be measured by how intelligent our machines become—it will be measured by how intelligently and compassionately we use those machines to shape our world.

# CHAPTER 9

# Building a Multicultural Family

## *Thoughts on Children*

AFTER YOU GET married, it's inevitable that people will start asking you about having kids. As I've grown older, I've learned about the many taboo topics that come with pregnancy, like miscarriages and postpartum depression. There are so many things no one teaches you in school, including the many changes that happen to your body during pregnancy and the postpartum period. Because I've never had children, none of my knowledge on this subject comes from personal experience; it's instead part of the prize that comes with waiting to start a family until later in life. If you follow in my footsteps, you too will get to watch your friends go through these life events first, and if you're lucky, your relationships will be strong enough that your friends will share with you the tough truths of it all as they go through their pregnancies. The reward is partially in the knowledge gained, and partially in the opportunity to be the best friend you can be by supporting a pregnant person through a complicated time.

I'll be honest: My knowledge about pregnancy was mostly learned after it was too late to be a supportive friend in real time. On two occasions, I was given the inside scoop about what was happening as it was happening, but I was too young and inexperienced to know how to be there to support my friends in the ways I might today. I hope I somehow provided some small amount of comfort to those friends, even in my ignorance.

Now, as I enter this phase of life for myself (i.e., married and considering children), I fear I know too much. Knowledge is power, but ignorance is bliss. I feel a level of worry I'm not sure I would have if I had been thinking about starting a family at a much younger age. When I think of having children, I begin thinking about all the things that could go wrong during pregnancy, and to be completely honest, I also think about the parts of my current life I'll have to give up to become a mother. My career, my ability to travel, and my quiet time with my husband—among many, many other things—will all be impacted by having children, so it's a heavy topic that weighs on me a lot.

Despite all those challenging considerations, I always thought I would become a mom. In fact, my desire to become a mother is the reason I'm not married to a different man today. My ex meant the world to me, but he had no desire to become a parent, and so we had to part ways. From there, my life evolved far differently than I imagined, and it's more beautiful than I ever could have imagined. I've done things I didn't know I could do, and I've been to places I didn't know existed. These opportunities were made possible in part because, for my entire adult life, I've only been responsible for myself.

There's a part of me that wants to keep seeing where my current path without kids will take me. However, I know I want to leave the world a better place, and I believe there is no better way to achieve that than to leave behind a legacy of strong moral values in a little package capable of living those values and sharing them with future generations. Now, that package could be a child I bear, one I adopt, one I foster... heck, I work in tech, so at this point, I might even consider an AI agent to be a part of my legacy. My legacy could be all these things and more, but the reality is bearing children is a journey for which your ticket to ride does, at a certain age, expire. So that leaves me where I am today, feeling pressure to make a decision, and also realizing that just wanting to have a child will not make it so.

When I think about who my child could be, I try to stay optimistic and say prayers of gratitude for the interconnected and opportunity-filled world they will enter into. It's a world where you can work from anywhere and learn for free to do almost anything. My child will hopefully not be made to choose which one ethnicity defines them, and they will see diversity in a whole new light. Perhaps they won't wrestle with identity questions as I have, and perhaps they won't be the only child of a unique racial makeup in their hometown. I don't know for sure if any of this will happen, but I can hope.

Because my husband is white and I am mixed, there is a decent chance my child will be fair-skinned. This could be advantageous in certain ways, but it may make things more complicated in other ways. Even with all the inner work I've done to become comfortable in my own skin, I know nothing can truly prepare me to guide the next generation through whatever is to come. Some days, it feels like we've come so far, but I'm also mindful of those who wish to halt or reverse the direction of our nation's progress towards equity and inclusion. As I said before, for me (or rather my identity), this *is* the greatest time to be an American, and I hope that will continue to be true for every generation that follows.

## The Words We Use

People say the strangest things sometimes. Years ago, I was at a bridal shower for a childhood friend at a local winery, and after many glasses of wine, one of the women attending asked me about the guy I had recently started dating. She wanted to see a photo of him, so I pulled out my phone and proudly showed her a picture of us together. The guy I had just started dating back then is now my husband, a fair-skinned man with a ginger beard. Her response to seeing the picture was immediate and not one I could have ever anticipated. Feeling very uninhibited from intoxication, she blurted out, "You two are going to have the most beautiful mulatto babies!"

I only knew the word *mulatto* from school history books, and I now know the word is listed in Webster's dictionary as "usually offensive." That day, the response in my mind was, "Did she just say what I think she said? What year are we in?!" Now, mind you, this woman is a handful of years younger than I am. If that statement had come from someone my own age, I still would have found it strange, but given the circumstances, hearing the term *mulatto* was even more shocking. And, while I know this woman had the best of intentions and meant to say something nice, her poor choice of words was what I walked away with, and I know I wasn't the only one. I may have been the only Black person at this gathering, but I certainly wasn't the only person who reacted with shock. No one actually voiced their opinion at the party, but the facial expressions from the other guests were enough to let me know I was not alone in my thoughts.

I truly believe this woman didn't know the word *mulatto* is an offensive term and reminiscent of when white male slave owners forced themselves on Black enslaved women, resulting in mixed-race children. This incident helps prove there is a problem with the way history was (and, in some schools today, still is) taught in our school systems. This also speaks to the power of colloquialism, and how certain words may not hold much meaning to some while they carry heavy baggage for others. For me, hearing the word *mulatto* conjured up a visceral reaction in the same way an African American might feel when stumbling upon an unexpected Confederate statue. (I say African American specifically because, as I discussed previously, not all Black people in America consider themselves African American.)

I have observed through my own social circles that white people don't talk about race nearly as much as Black people do, so a lack of knowledge among many white people is inevitable. Black people are always talking about race because it affects them inherently—every day and in every way—and it can't be escaped. The implications of race are everywhere, constantly playing a role in the way we move through the world. My father-in-law has expressed to me how thankful he is to have had the opportunity to get to know me and my family because it has opened his eyes to a different way of seeing the world. I think this is especially true because my dad talks about race continually, likely without even realizing it. I'm sure he would be all too glad to never have to mention race again, but it's ingrained in him to see how race affects the way he is perceived in any situation.

There is so much racial terminology that even as someone who grew up in a household where race was talked about all the time, there was (and likely still is) so much more for me to learn. For example, when I was in my late twenties, I attended an outdoor event close to where I grew up, and I stopped to order lunch from a local food truck. There was a Black gentleman staffing the truck's window, and his first question to me was, "Where are your folks from?" As this had happened to me many times before, I assumed he knew my dad or my grandparents, so I told him the town where my dad is from. His face lit up with a knowing smile as he said, "Yeah, I knew it, because you're one of them redbones." Feeling a bit creeped out, I decided not to order anything and remove myself from that particular situation, partly because I didn't know what the word *redbone* meant.

I called my dad to tell him about the incident, and he laughed before explaining to me that "redbone" refers to a light-skinned Black person. Apparently, the area my dad is from is known for having a high population of light-skinned Black women, which attracted many male suitors to the area. (Lighter skin is often seen as desirable by many in the Black community.) I felt justified in the creepy vibe I got from the man in the food truck, and I was glad I chose to walk away in search of another lunch option.

## Learning Malay

While working at the resort on Sibu Island, I wanted to learn some basic Malay, in part to be able to interact more with the villagers, but also in part to be able to communicate with family members when I would finally get to Penang to meet my mom's extended family. I was excited to get more in touch with this side of my heritage, especially as the only language I had ever spoken with members of my mom's family in the States was English.

When I arrived with my mom and sister in Penang, I quickly remembered the language I should have been studying was a Chinese dialect called Hokkien. My mom had once mentioned to me that while growing up, she spoke English at school, Malay around town, and Hokkien at home. It was a detail I had forgotten until arriving in Penang, when I realized my limited but intentionally learned Malay vocabulary wasn't going to get me very far.

I understand why people forego their native languages when they move to the US. Proficiency in the English language will take you far, and practice makes perfect. However, there is certainly a part of me that wishes I had learned some Hokkien growing up. It could have been like a fun code language to use with my sister when we were out and about that surely no one in our hometown would have understood.

There are benefits to learning a second language at an early age. It enhances core cognitive skills, such as reasoning, problem solving, and memory. It makes you a stronger communicator. While I feel as though I am pretty advanced in these areas, I still wish I had learned another language earlier in life. At this age, I find it quite hard to grasp language-learning, and I wonder what being raised as a bilingual child might have been like.

## Community

Diversity in my community is important to me. Growing up in an area with very little diversity, then moving to one of the most diverse cities on the planet, showed me I thrive in diverse communities. My life feels much more enriched when I am constantly interacting with people of varied backgrounds who can offer perspectives different from my own, perspectives that I can learn and grow from. Within that diversity, there may also be folks who share my perspectives on certain topics, which is important to my mental well-being so that I feel I'm not alone in the way I perceive and internalize interactions or events.

As I've said, I grew up having the same friends from kindergarten through high school graduation, and I'm still friends with some of these people today. There's nothing that can replace the closeness you feel with people who have known you for your entire life. In that way, there's something special about being from a small town. When I was in elementary school, a song by Tracy Byrd came out. It was titled, "I'm from the Country," and the lyrics describe my childhood: "Everybody knows everybody. Everybody calls you friend. You don't need an invitation, kick off your shoes, come on in." That was the country environment I grew up in.

Oddly enough, I grew up feeling comfortable in a place where no one looked like me. But that was in my childhood, largely in a non-digital age. Today, having experienced places in the world with more diversity, I've come to realize a different and sometimes deeper level of community is possible. This deeper connection is often cultivated online through the exchange of diverse perspectives, cultures, and experiences, which enrich our understanding and empathy for one another. In diverse communities, there's often a greater need to explain why things are done in a certain way, as shared traditions and assumptions can't be taken for granted. This openness fosters inclusivity and creates vibrant communities where everyone feels valued and has the opportunity to contribute meaningfully. When I think about the beautiful places I've visited and might like to live one day—like Vermont and Oregon—I can't help but wonder if I would feel fulfilled by the local community there, given the lack of diversity I observed during my time in those places.

I think about the future, and about possibly having children one day. Do I want my kids to grow up the way I grew up? Will it be enough for them to have lasting friendships with good people, even if these good people cannot relate to my children's experiences navigating the world as individuals of a unique racial and ethnic makeup? Will such concerns even matter for that next generation? With the advent of the internet, smartphones, and social media, and with our constant level of connectivity, will the young people of the next generation view the world in a new light and think of community differently because this digital age allows for connections in ways that my more-analog childhood did not?

What I do know is that if I have children, I would like my husband and I to plant our roots somewhere before they begin school, and then stay there for as long as we can, to give them the continuity of community that I had. Strong, lasting community ties, even with people I was ethnically different from, built in me a sense of belonging. My dad had that same kind of upbringing, with the same schools and same friends throughout his primary school and high school experiences. In fact, his younger sister (my aunt) is now working on a project to restore an old African American schoolhouse in their hometown, the one my grandma went to. Today, the schoolhouse requires a great deal of restoration work, and my aunt is on a mission to ensure the building is brought back to life as an education and community center.

She's also helping older community members who attended the schoolhouse as children preserve their history for future generations. I think it's a rare and special experience to know and connect with whole families, including multiple generations of a given family, and that's what growing up with strong ties to a community allows for.

My husband had a more transient childhood, and when we go to events in my hometown or my dad's hometown, he's always fascinated by the number of people who have lived there for their entire lives. I always have stories to tell about how people are related or connected, whether it be through school, work, church, extracurricular activities, or otherwise. Each time is a walk down memory lane for me, and most often, it's an enjoyable one.

# CHAPTER 10

# Looking Forward

*Perpetuating Stereotypes*

I STAYED BUSY with activities as a kid, and I was constantly juggling a packed schedule that often left me running late as I hopped from one place to another. During these formative years of my life, I heard about the concept of "CP time" (i.e., "Colored People's time"), which is a stereotype referring to Black people always being late. As I got older, I noticed my own confirmation bias at play—confirmation bias being the tendency to seek and interpret information in ways that confirm pre-existing beliefs. I began to associate the CP time stereotype with my own tardiness along with my observations of others' tardiness.

I only recently learned the term *CP time* has historical roots as a form of resistance. During slavery and segregation, strict adherence to mainstream timeframes often reflected power dynamics and control, whereas Black communities created their own rhythms and time practices for social gatherings and events. At Black churches, celebrations, and gatherings, the focus is often on community connection and engagement rather than rigid punctuality.

This more fluid approach to time is common in some countries. For instance, in Latin America, there is a concept called

❧

*la hora Latina,* which refers to start times for casual gatherings beginning one hour later than what is listed on the invitation. In Latin American countries, this is the norm and carries no stigma, but in the US, CP time is an inherently Black stereotype rooted in a complex interplay of history, culture, and systemic factors. While we often hear CP time used as lighthearted humor, its origins reveal a deeper story of resistance and autonomy. It's disappointing but not surprising to me to see how those resistance efforts have been misconstrued to perpetuate stereotypes of inefficiency and irresponsibility.

The stereotype may be pervasive, but one thing I can tell you is CP time never applied to my dad, as he's always been early to everything. My habit of tardiness definitely did *not* come from him, as he always had us together and ready to go on time— when going out with my dad, you are a reflection of him, and punctual you will be. For my sister and me, being punctual was a fairly easy way to avoid getting into trouble, and we acted accordingly. These days, while I try to be as communicative as possible if I'm running late, I hate the idea of perpetuating a stereotype. Although, I'm not entirely sure if my running late *actually* perpetuates the stereotype, because most people don't really think of me as being Black.

Another stereotype I think a lot about is the Asian tourist who takes pictures of everything. I would be lying if I said the thought doesn't cross my mind often when traveling. I love taking photos so I can better remember all the amazing moments and people in my life, and I have pictures from around the globe. In fact, when my aunt gave me a selfie stick for Christmas at the height of their popularity, I was initially excited. However, I soon became hesitant to use it: I didn't want to be seen as a typical Asian tourist.

While people of all ethnicities take photos when traveling, Asian tourists are often associated with taking numerous photos of landmarks, food, and even seemingly mundane objects. The economic growth of Japan, China, and South Korea in the 1980s and 1990s led to an influx of Asian travel groups, making their tourist behaviors more prominently visible during my childhood and teenage years. Movies, television shows, and advertisements reinforced these stereotypes through exaggerated characters, embedding them into my mind as something to be cognizant of during my own travels. Of course, I would still take photos on my trips, but I always tried my best not to call attention to myself.

Eventually I grew out of this paranoia, and now I embrace every opportunity to take fun photos of places, faces, and moments I want to remember. I can't exactly attribute this mental shift to any particular event, but in early adulthood I began taking jumping photos on trips with friends, which is anything but discreet in nature. The energy and excitement captured in each jumping photo was worth the uninvited attention, in my opinion. Who knows, I might even have inspired others to get a bit more creative with their own photos.

I'm sure how we are perceived by others is something we all think about and struggle with, regardless of race. While that may be true, there's a compounding impact when there are multiple layers of identity at play. These layers may be related to being two or more ethnicities, but this may also be related to the plethora of additional identities with which someone can associate themselves. (Other identities that come to mind include gender, sexual identity, height, weight, and age, just to name a few.) We spend so much time worrying about what others will think based on assumptions, preconceived notions, and unconscious biases, when, in reality, it's unlikely anyone even notices whatever trait it is that we're self-conscious about.

It has taken me decades to have this epiphany, and the way it came about was not even related to social anxiety—it was just an everyday moment. My husband asked me what he wore out to dinner a few nights earlier because he couldn't find his wallet. I then realized I had no idea what he wore. From that small revelation, I came to recognize that all the time I'd spent in my life hemming and hawing over what to wear was likely unnecessary: Very few people pay enough attention to notice when you repeat an outfit, and even fewer care if your shoes perfectly match your dress. Extrapolating further, I began to ponder the multitude of things we stress over but that almost no one else notices, like the small pimple on your chin or the fleeting comment you made in casual conversation. Similarly, I realized actions I fear might reinforce stereotypes are often not as significant to others as they feel to me. Most people aren't watching all that closely, let alone connecting a single action to a sweeping generalization about an entire group. Sometimes, when we think we are representing an entire group of people, we are really only representing ourselves.

I acknowledge stereotypes are very real, and I don't want to downplay the idea that stereotypes come about for a reason. When there are behaviors that have been noticed repeatedly among the same racial group, generalizations are created that are not always accurate and often could apply to anyone. For example, not all Asian people are good at math, and not all Black people are naturally athletic. Those talents are not specific to those groups, nor are they applicable to all people within those groups. The point I'm making is that open conversations about stereotypes and the harm they cause are much more likely to have an impact against their pervasiveness than my speeding to ensure I'm on time (one person, one time), or missing out on taking a photo of an awesome vacation memory. Instead of overthinking these things on my own, I should speak up and start open dialogues with others. We often project our thoughts onto others, assuming stereotypes are being applied to us, when in reality, that might not be the case at all.

## We've Come a Long Way

There are so many products on the market now that simply didn't exist when I was growing up. These items shouldn't be taken for granted because they are evidence of a cultural shift, one that values people across the racial spectrum. I'm going to highlight just a few products here, because the list is quite extensive.

I've touched on this already, but as a curly girl the amount of choice I now have in hair products has grown tremendously. As a child, I struggled with hair products and hairdressers, but in college, I learned about DevaChan salons, which specialized in curly hair and had their own line of curl-friendly products. While all DevaChan salons are now closed, their DevaCurl products can be found at many major retailers, such as Target and CVS, whereas for a long time they were only for sale in the salon or at specialty beauty shops. Even more exciting is that DevaCurl is now among many other curly-focused brands, like Carol's Daughter, Rizos Curls, and Ouidad, just to name a few. The amount of choice I have in haircare products is both overwhelming and empowering. I love my curls, and I love that I can now easily find (and afford) products to help them be happy and healthy.

In that same vein, because my mom often had no idea what to do with my hair, I wish YouTube and its many tutorials for curly-haired people had existed when I was a kid. (YouTube was created in 2005, once I was already in college.) While my mom might not have been able to benefit from *all* the curly hair tutorials which exist now, I can and do—even now as an adult in my thirties—still try to figure out the best ways to style my hair. I have watched a variety of styling tutorials on both YouTube and Instagram. We shouldn't take for granted all the things we can learn from crowd-sourced content-platforms such as these—class is held in the comfort of our homes and at no cost!

Today, the possibilities of learning from these platforms are great. To all the curly kid moms out there, I couldn't be more excited for you. And to all the curly kids around the globe, may you be spared the world of pain associated with so-called "tender headedness," which I experienced as a child whenever I went to the salon. Thankfully, today the world is more educated, and the scalps of children everywhere are better for it.

Other items I have enjoyed watching come to store shelves are inclusive products to match a variety of skin tones. I have a vivid memory of dressing up as Jasmine from Disney's *Aladdin* for Halloween as a child. The costume was Jasmine's most well-known outfit from the film, a turquoise midriff top and harem pants. Costumes in the 1990s were much more modest than they are today, and so my outfit was a one-piece costume with a "nude" or "skin-colored" piece of fabric sewn between the top and pants. As you can imagine, the color of the fabric was not a skin tone that matched mine, and for that reason, the costume was less than ideal. (Notably, Jasmine's ethnicity should have made the skin-colored piece of fabric much closer to my own skin tone, but I guess the costume's manufacturers had a different customer in mind.) I knew the costume looked a little odd on me, but the alternative was not dressing up as Jasmine at all. Despite the mismatch, my desire to be a Disney princess outweighed any concerns about the costume.

Today, products are evolving to include a spectrum of skin tones. Along the same lines as the Jasmine costume, pantyhose are now available in a range of colors to better match various complexions. For a long time, pantyhose came in one shade of "nude" that was supposed to work for everyone, no matter how dark or light your skin was. Likewise, undergarments are now made in a range of skin tones as well, to make it easier to camouflage them under clothes made of thin or semi-sheer materials. Even adhesive bandages can be bought in a color closer to your own skin tone now, when for a long time there was only one shade available.

A fun, but important, product I came upon more recently is colored pencils in a variety of skin tones. This is so important! For kids, seeing themselves in their activity books is crucial to their development and sense of self-worth. To be able to accurately color in their drawings or coloring books, using their own skin tone, proves they are seen and valued by society. Children may not experience this inclusiveness all that profoundly in the moment, but subconsciously they will pick up on it. These things matter. Take it from someone who had to blend shades or color with a crayon ever-so-lightly to try to reflect her own skin tone on a page. No combination of yellow, orange, and brown ever came close to representing how I saw myself, but today a single colored pencil can solve this problem.

## Music & Film

One of my girlfriends once said to me, "You know we Black people always have to have music playing." While I doubt this is true for every Black person in America, it does adequately describe many Black people I know and grew up with. One of my fondest memories is singing Whitney Houston's version of "I'm Every Woman" at the top of my lungs with my aunts and cousins after opening presents together on Christmas. Maybe the song wasn't a traditional Christmas carol, but we sang it with the conviction of true feminists in the same way we would've sung "Silent Night" with the conviction of true Christians.

Like most, my early musical tastes were formed by the people around me. So, while I listened to K95 country radio so I could keep up with the latest hits like the kids at school, at home my dad played the hits of Motown alongside some more contemporary R&B. Each genre made me feel connected to different, yet equally important, parts of my life, and both brought me immense joy.

My dad loves music. In his garage, he still has his old stereo system, complete with his 8-track player, a cassette tape deck, a record player, and speakers. In high school, I remember being asked on various occasions to burn multiple copies of the same CD for him to ensure he had a dedicated copy for each of his vehicles. While you probably won't ever catch him dancing, you can always see him smiling when a favorite song of his comes on. If the music was playing softly when we were riding in the car and a song he liked came on the radio, he'd turn up the volume without hesitation, wanting us all to enjoy it together. These days, he's more of a backseat passenger when we're in the car together, but he still asks me to turn up the volume from time to time.

As I got older, the kids at school became more eclectic in their tastes. Of course, boy bands had their moment in my life, as was confirmed by the New Kids on the Block poster my sister proudly hung on her wall. Emo music also had its moment, supplying me with overly emotional, passive-aggressive lyrics to post on my AOL Instant Messenger away messages. Then hip-hop and rap music slid their way into the rotation via pop radio. This was mostly before you could look up song lyrics on the internet, so I'm sure the number of songs I sang along to as a child with completely incorrect lyrics far outweighed the number of songs with lyrics I fully understood.

When I got to college to study music business, I quickly learned there were whole segments of famous American artists and music I'd had no exposure to at all. Billy Joel, Bruce Springsteen, Bob Dylan... the list goes on. These are names that I recognized but not ones to which I could attribute songs, nor could

I sing along to most of their hits. It was weird to be enrolled in one of the top (and at that time, one of the only) music business programs in the country while being unable to identify some of the industry's most iconic recordings. These were the hits from before my time, and if I hadn't learned them from my parents at home or from the kids at school, where else would I have learned them?

My mom might have grown up overseas in Malaysia, but just to demonstrate the pervasiveness of American music throughout the globe, my mom chose her American name of Priscilla based on her knowledge of Priscilla Presley, Elvis Presley's wife. Mom grew up on American music, but she wasn't much of a music fan. It wasn't until I was in college that I learned her favorite band growing up was Santana. She had never mentioned it, and rarely did she choose the music we listened to at home or in the car—she was happy to bop along to whatever tunes someone else put on.

I do wish there were more crossover artists from other countries into mainstream music. While working in New York City after college, I volunteered for a music festival called globalFEST, which served as my first real exposure to international music. An array of artists from across the globe played on multiple stages over two or three nights at Webster Hall in the East Village. Today, globalFEST continues on a larger scale at the famed Lincoln Center, but I believe the festival and the artists it promotes still don't have the reach they deserve. Personally, I'm always so glad to see international artists brought to my town via the annual Richmond Folk Festival, and I hope other cities have similar events which introduce people to music from other parts of the world. In this current era dominated by music streaming, maybe international music will become more prevalent in American society than before, when we all had to rely on traditional radio to direct us to the latest and greatest in music.

My experience with films is a lot like my experience with music. Until I was an adult, I didn't realize my exposure differed from other people's. Two of my favorite movies of all time are *Love & Basketball* and *Brown Sugar*, both films which feature majority-Black casts. I have watched both many times, and anyone who knows me knows I rarely watch anything more than once. (Sitting still in front of a television is not my first pick for a leisure activity.) In the same way that some of my music business classmates couldn't believe I didn't know the hits of the Rolling Stones, I always feel a sense of astonishment when learning someone hasn't seen either of my favorite films. I'm told these two movies are both Black films, but I never thought of them that way—I simply consider them quality entertainment.

The release of the Marvel Studios film *Black Panther* was probably the first majority-Black-cast film I recognized as a blockbuster hit. It's a film that, undeniably, almost anyone would recognize if I brought it up in conversation. That movie came out when I was in my early thirties, so I think a lot about how many amazing films many people have missed because Black movies have not historically made it into mainstream culture.

Similarly, *Crazy Rich Asians* was the first majority-Asian-cast film I recognized as a blockbuster hit that wasn't stereotypically focused on martial arts. This romantic comedy, released in 2018, came out well into my adult years. Prior to that film, I could only name *Crouching Tiger, Hidden Dragon* and

*Mulan* as majority-Asian blockbusters. The former is the most successful non-English-language film in the US (so it's not an American film), and the latter is an animated Disney movie. Talk about a lack of representation! That's not to say other similar films didn't exist, but they certainly were never on my radar.

I'm thankful for my early exposure to Black American cinema, and I'm curious to explore other types of films like Bollywood (Indian) or Nollywood (Nigerian) movies. Diversity leads to access and exposure, which leads to knowledge and understanding. This fuels innovation, creativity, collaboration, and so much more. To have a family who can introduce you to various types of media is a blessing, and it's a spark that can ignite your curiosity to explore even further. I'm thankful for the eclectic taste I have in music and films, and I hope I will continue to inspire others to diversify their interests as well.

## How Will We Measure?

Sometimes I just want to say, "Stop asking me to identify my race!" every time a survey pops up. Choosing one race over the other makes me uncomfortable, and I loathed having to do it in my earlier years. Today, there are options on surveys that don't force me to choose, but what are we going to do with this new data? What I mean is, if I select "Other" or "Biracial" or "Two or More Races," of what use is that data?

I understand it's important for us to collect data on race if we want to right the wrongs of the past. In order to track progress, we must continue to track metrics. Without the collection of this data, how can we know if we are closing the wealth gap?

How can we identify disparities in education or home owner-
ship or numerous other things? Since we've expanded on the
options to select for racial identity, the question I wonder about
is: Are we still collecting useful information? If I mark that I am
"Two or More Races" on a survey, but I don't state what those
races are, has any useful information really been collected? If
I'm Caucasian and Asian, I might choose "Biracial" on a form,
as might someone who is Black and Hispanic. These are different things, but there's rarely an option on a survey to specifically
state one's races and ethnicities if selecting more than one. Depending on the subject being measured, it's likely the additional
data regarding the races are important so that the data can reflect
a more accurate picture.

There are so many young people of mixed race that are
about to skew the statistics on everything from income levels to
homeownership as they become adults, and I hope we're collecting the correct information to be able to continue to do the work
of closing disparity gaps while still acknowledging the complete
identities of all people.

## *Talking Politics*

Politics can be such a divisive topic. I admit I'm not a huge
fan of our two-party system and the way that it pits Americans
against each other, but that's the system we have. There are other flaws in this system, too, including how racially charged it is.
When I was growing up, I could sense race loomed large in the
political arena, and sadly, it still feels that way today.

In elementary school, we took an assessment that was intended to tell us which political party we were most closely aligned with based on our views on various topics. This was so many years ago that I don't remember any of the questions, but what I do remember is the assessment informed me I leaned Republican. This was a huge shock for me, as I had always known I was a Democrat. Both my parents were Democrats, my understanding was that all Black people are Democrats, and I was told the Democratic party most closely represented our interests. Imagine my surprise when I took an *academic* assessment that informed me I aligned with the opposite political party from my parents.

In hindsight, I'm not sure I trust the accuracy of the assessment given the times and the region of my school, but I'm thankful for something else I learned. I realized that without looking at the issues and the platforms of individual candidates, you are not fully prepared to cast your ballot. The idea that your party will always be aligned with your beliefs is not true. Leadership changes. The economy changes. Culture changes. You have to pay attention and be an active participant in the process of democracy if you intend to have a say in those changes. This is not to say I have always been good at this, or that I follow each political candidate closely, but I'm aware groupthink will get us nowhere. I must evaluate every election on its own terms, and I must examine every candidate on their own individual merits and platform.

It's amazing the way political propaganda can lead people to believe a candidate has their best interest at heart, despite that candidate's history and public stance on divisive issues.

I remember getting into a heated argument with my mom's mom—my own grandma—over a particularly contentious political candidate who she believed was the right person for the job for reasons which did not match his track record at all. My attempt to have a civil conversation while asking questions and giving facts to counter what she thought to be true didn't go so well, and that was the last time she and I ever talked politics. While communication is the key to understanding, sometimes people just aren't open to the conversation. In this instance, it was more important to me to preserve the relationship with a woman I loved and respected, which is possible to do even when you don't agree politically.

All this is to say: We should make no assumptions about someone's political views, and we should respect the choices of others. We should be grateful to live in a country where we have the freedom to choose our leaders. It's a right many people in the world don't have, so to assume our own political alignments based on the affiliations of those around us—without researching candidates ourselves each election cycle—is to take this privilege for granted. Politically speaking, my extended families differed in their allegiances, and luckily that (along with the party-affiliation exercise in elementary school) taught me early on to pay less attention to generalizations and more attention to individuals and facts. I think about politics in much the same way I think about my race: I can identify as more than one race, and I can agree with either political party on any given issue. Political parties, like race, are a social construct. We must elect the best person for the position every time, and that person can come from either side of the aisle and from any background.

## President Obama

In 2008, Barack Obama won the election for his first presidential term. I was living in New York City. It quickly became a running joke that if my friends and I had any trouble getting into events, restaurants, or bars, I would simply say to the doorman, "My Uncle Barack will be so disappointed to hear we were treated this way!" I never actually did it, but I always thought it would be funny to try to see if it would work.

The world saw Obama as the first Black president, but let's acknowledge he was also the first biracial president—something he talked about freely. His rise to the highest seat of power in the country, and arguably the world, meant so much to so many people. His message of hope and change resonated with a wide spectrum of people, including young people, people of color, and others who felt disconnected from traditional political elites. For many, his victory represented the realization of the American dream, evidencing that a Black man could rise to the highest office in the land, which was especially powerful in the context of our country's history of slavery, segregation, and racial inequality. Obama's election marked a transformative moment in American history and symbolized the possibility of progress, equity, and opportunity for all Americans. As someone who hadn't seen a lot of mixed-race leaders or had many mixed-race role models, this was monumental for me.

I certainly began to pay more attention to politics once Obama began his campaign for his first term as president, and my enthusiasm for politics didn't wane after he was elected. I was just as attentive during his run for his second term, and I noticed a lot of my friends—friends of all races—taking more of an interest in politics as well. I even had one friend who, inspired by Obama, ran for city council in New York City. It's amazing what the right leadership can do to motivate people to not just take interest, but to take action.

It's important for young people to be able to see people who look like them achieving great success, so they can then imagine themselves in those same positions. While I don't have any political aspirations myself, I do find hope and motivation in seeing people of color rise through the ranks of government. I'm still patiently waiting for a female president, but I will take what I can get in the meantime. A multiracial woman such as Kamala Harris as the vice president was a good start. Knowing that someone who looks like me—and, by that, I mean Harris is racially ambiguous (because certainly not all people of mixed heritage look alike)—can be elected to such an elite position of power is encouraging and exciting. So much of the population is mixed race now that it's inevitable we will see more and more of this, but I think it's important to acknowledge where we are today and celebrate those who are paving the way.

## Bringing the Neighborhood Together

If you flip the perspective of feeling as though you don't belong to any one group, you might then view life through the lens of belonging to every group. This is how I approached life from a very young age. I believed, even then, that there was no place where I didn't belong. I still feel that way on most days, even now. I'm honestly not sure where this confidence came from, but I have been fortunate to be able to quickly ignore and forget the times when I have been excluded from groups or activities for superfluous reasons. I'm not saying it hasn't happened, but I am saying I have made a choice not to let it define me or hold me back. I guess it's a perk of having a quick-moving mind ... I'm always on to the next thing.

This was not something I realized about myself until recently, when I was talking to a friend who was reflecting on her own experiences. She and I had been attending a local line dancing class at the community center in our neighborhood. This was not country line dancing, but what I refer to as R&B line dancing. Think less Cotton-Eyed Joe and more Cha-Cha Slide, less Watermelon Crawl and more Cupid Shuffle. I grew up country line dancing in school, and when I was doing my graduate summer internship just outside of Nashville, TN, I felt right at home line dancing at Murph's Country Barn. But I also love a good R&B line dance—it has a bit more groove and style to it—so I really enjoyed this particular class.

While talking to my friend, a white female, she said she would only attend the dance classes on nights when I was going as well. We are residents of a predominantly Black neighborhood, and the participants in the line dancing class were all Black—and they were mostly women over fifty, too. My friend expressed that she would never go alone into what appeared to be a safe space for the Black community of our neighborhood, and while I understood her sentiment, I was glad I could be a conduit for her to have a lens into the lifeblood of our community so that she could get to know the residents who lived there.

It's important to note I *like* being a conduit between people who might not normally cross paths. I *like* taking my friends with me into situations they might not normally experience. This isn't something I feel obligated to do, but it's truly something I enjoy because diversity of experience is important. It's eye-opening and character-building, and it's also often quite fun! I say this because the role of conduit is not for everyone, and no one should feel they *have* to do this work. I build bridges because I want to, but I also know that for many people this type of work is uncomfortable and/or exhausting, and that's okay too—I'm happy to lighten their loads. Bringing people together is no one's burden to carry alone, and for those who don't feel energized by this work, trust there are others like me who enjoy it.

To that point, not everyone views an opportunity for connecting cultures in the same way. Five years ago, when I told a friend where I was buying a house after putting in the offer, his immediate response was, "You know you're now a gentrifier, right?" He said it in jest, but I knew there was truth to his comment. It was something I hadn't considered, and it filled me with guilt, even though I'm a Black woman. Gentrification often means displacement, and I didn't want to contribute to that narrative. I think about that all the time, and I try to be mindful of how my presence affects those who live around me. I understand the reality that if I hadn't bought the house, the new owner would probably have been another gentrifier. So, while I can't stop further gentrification in my neighborhood, what I *can* do— as a person who feels comfortable getting to know *all* my neighbors—is help bring old neighbors and new neighbors together.

Bringing people together can also mean simply showing up. Every year I attend a community breakfast put on by a nonprofit that has operated in my neighborhood for many years. The president & CEO of the organization is a friend. She's not from the neighborhood, but she tries hard to bring the community together. One of the ways she brings her volunteers, those they serve, and other area residents together is through this annual breakfast. I look forward to it every year, and I always meet new neighbors when I go—and these are people I likely wouldn't meet otherwise.

I think my blended background has helped me to feel comfortable around a variety of cultures, and I will always try to help those in my social circle who are without that kind of confidence and/or curiosity feel the same. Again, not everyone is suited to this work, and that's okay, but I'm grateful to be able to help connect others, whether it's by something big, like making a conscious choice to invite my white friends into a Black space, or it's through something as small as starting a conversation with a neighbor.

# Outro

## *Layers*

THE STORIES AND perspectives in this book focus on how race and culture have shaped my life, but the truth is we all have various layers that make up who we are. I am Black and Asian, but I am also female, petite, left-handed, and the youngest child in my family. These characteristics, among others, all have implications for how I navigate through the world and how I am perceived by others.

Each layer is like a subculture we are a part of. These layers influence the way we think, talk, dress, and react in various situations. While not everyone can relate to my experiences of being Black or Asian, I do believe everyone can relate to struggling with the parts of their identity that don't quite seem to match.

I hope everyone can see themselves in at least one story I've shared, because we are all walking through this life wrestling with the various pieces that make up the puzzle of our identity. There is certainly more that connects us through our experiences as humans than there are things which make us different. As time goes on and the world becomes more connected, we will only continue to see cultures blend and societies evolve. I'm proud to be a part of today's wave of that movement, and I'm thankful for the character it has built in me.

The title of this book, *Blackinese,* came from the playground of my elementary school. The word came out of the mouth of a little boy who grew up to be one of my best friends. He didn't call me Blackinese with malicious intent ... the word was just his way of explaining my racial and cultural makeup to others. He saw both parts of me, and it's only in my adult years that I've come to appreciate how special that was for someone at such a young age. May we all venture through life with attentive hearts that acknowledge people fully for who they are, because there's so much more to each person than just what our eyes can see.

# Acknowledgments

First, I want to thank *you* for picking up this book. There are countless ways you could be spending your time, and I am deeply honored that you chose my words and stories in this moment.

To everyone who helped make this book possible—whether you proofread a section, let me bounce ideas off you, or simply encouraged me along the way—I am forever grateful for your time, insight, and support.

*To Alex:*
Your vulnerable and sometimes brutally honest feedback has been invaluable. You always approach critique with care, and you're never afraid to tell me if something feels off. Thank you for helping me present the most authentic version of myself. I love you beyond words.

*To Mom:*
Thank you for allowing me to explore the many possibilities of who and what I could be from a young age. I also want to thank you for encouraging me to enter scholarship essay contests. While the goal then might have been for financial aid, those experiences laid the foundation for my writing journey without which this book likely would not have been possible.

*To Dad:*
Thank you for always being unapologetically true to who you are. You've always been a shining example for me of both integrity and authenticity. I'm grateful for the many lessons you continue to teach me every day with both care and humor.

*To Cass:*
Thank you for being the best big sister and role model. You let me watch and learn from your every step through life, and I don't know where I'd be without you.

*To Cheats:*
Thank you for inviting me to write an essay for the project *Voices: Critical Thought in a Challenging Time.* That project inspired me to expand those early pages into the full memoir you're now holding. Your encouragement was the spark I needed.

*To Nadia and Linzy:*
Our tradition of setting yearly intentions gave me the focus I needed. In 2024, my guiding word was "book," and it pushed me to finally finish this manuscript. Thank you for holding me accountable.

*To the James River Writers Association:*
Thank you for being both a resource and a supportive community I could lean on.

*To the "I Need an Editor" Facebook group:*
Thank you for leading me to Erika's Editing. Erika DeSimone, your work brought polish and depth to this book. Your thoughtful questions made me dig deeper, and I can't thank you enough for your dedication.

*To the Fairfield–Henrico County Public Library:*
Your cozy fireplace area provided the perfect setting for writing and editing. A special thanks to my friend Jana for introducing me to this gem and for working alongside me in silent support.

*To the Google Docs app on my phone:*
Your offline capabilities allowed me to write and edit while flying around the world. You made productivity possible in unexpected places.

*Most importantly, to God:*
Thank you for blessing me with this incredible, messy, wonderful life and all the people in it. Your constant presence has helped me see the good in the world and find silver linings in the darkest moments. Thank you for guiding me and teaching me the lessons I share in these pages. I'm also grateful to The Life Church RVA for re-sharing my sermon notes each Sunday (which look a lot like the doodles that divide each section of this book). Those moments remind me that words have power and are meant to be shared.

# About the Author

*Photo Credit: Andrew Levine*

Patricia Bradby Moore is a proud multi-hyphenate who refuses to be defined by a single label. She is a writer, keynote speaker, connectivity coach, technologist, voiceover artist, community builder, traveler, runner, swimmer, cyclist, scuba diver, and amateur ukulele player. Patricia is passionate about using her experience and expertise to help others embrace every facet of their identity and live their most fulfilling lives. She views her versatility as a superpower—one that fuels innovation and builds a happier, more connected world.

Learn more at www.patriciabmoore.com, and connect with her on Instagram @patricia.b.moore.